The cookbook
for guys
who want to
impress girls
but have little equipment and even less experience

© 2007 Rebo International
This edition: © 2007 Rebo Productions b.v., Lisse

www.rebo-publishers.com
info@rebo-publishers.com

Text: Nicole Seeman
Photography: Raphaële Vidaling
Design: Claire Guigal
Original title: Le livre de cuisine pour les garçons qui veulent épater les filles avec peu de
matériel et encore moins d'expérience
© 2006 Copyright SA, 12, Villa de Loucine, 75014, Paris, France
Translation: First Edition Ltd, Cambridge, UK
Editing: Sarah Dunham, Erin Slattery

ISBN: 978-90-366-2177-9

The cookbook
for guys
who want to
impress girls
but have little equipment and even less experience

Text: Nicole Seeman
Photographs: Raphaële Vidaling

Contents

Be sure to read this before you begin, or you'll turn into a pumpkin at midnight!

Main dishes

Accompaniments

Desserts

Breakfast

Introduction

It is sometimes said that the shortest way to a man's heart is via his stomach. Well, that's even more true of a woman! Preparing a meal for the girl you especially want to impress shows her you are generous, attentive, creative, not macho... The ideal sort of guy, half Superman, half Santa Claus. Well worth the effort, wouldn't you say? The restful atmosphere of dinner for two, at your place; what better way of seducing her? But there's just one problem: you're not a brilliant cook, even your knowledge of things culinary is hazy, your experience is practically zero, and you think getting some fast food delivered would be quite good enough. Don't fool yourself. The book you are about to read is your secret weapon.

The heart of the woman of your dreams will be won among the pots and pans.

In this book, you will find...

- plenty of recipes for two:
    - very straightforward and virtually foolproof
      (having said that, no one is perfect);
    - which will make an impression
      (she'll see you've taken some trouble);
    - which are just right for girls
      (more creamed chicken than fish stew) ;
    - chosen with your limited kitchen equipment in mind
      (no need for a complicated vegetable slicer, fancy mixing bowl, or multi functional food processor);
    - with clear instructions
      (a degree in languages is not essential!);
    - without too many complicated ingredients
      (I see! Your Mom amd Pop store doesn't sell Jerusalem artichokes?);
    - with useful information on where to get things
      (no, you won't find coconut milk in the dairy section of the supermarket).

- recipes classified according to the type of girl you have invited;

- and, as a bonus, if the evening extends into morning, some advice on preparing a nice breakfast.

The equipment you need for these recipes

This list includes only kitchen equipment. If you are thinking of having someone around for dinner, you must obviously have silverware, plates, glasses... (if not, you'd better fall back on a pizza delivered in a cardboard box; all you need in that case is a telephone).

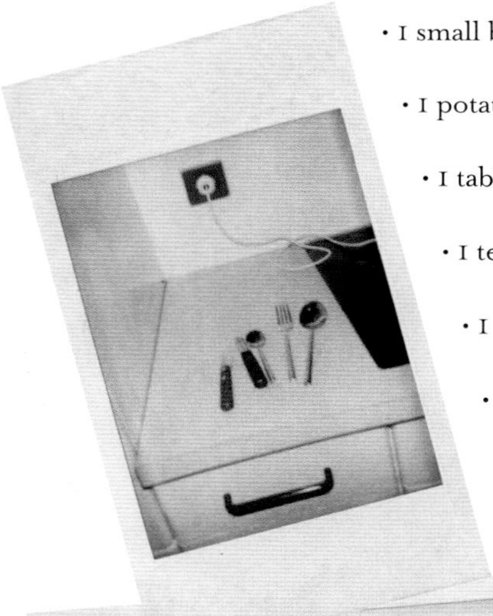

- 1 small but sharp kitchen knife

- 1 potato peeler

- 1 tablespoon

- 1 teaspoon

- 1 fork

- 1 measuring cup (holding about 8 ounces)

- sheets or a roll of baking parchment (to keep food from sticking to the pan when baking)

- 1 small bowl (the size of a breakfast cereal bowl) for mixing things

- 1 salad bowl

- 1 stove (gas, electric, or other)

- 1 nonstick skillet

- 1 spatula for turning the food while it is cooking without spoiling it or scratching the frying pan

- 2 saucepans (you might just get by with one)

- I oven

- I baking tray or ovenproof broiler pan

- I ovenproof dish for 2 persons

- I (thick) dish towel or oven glove for handling the hot dishes

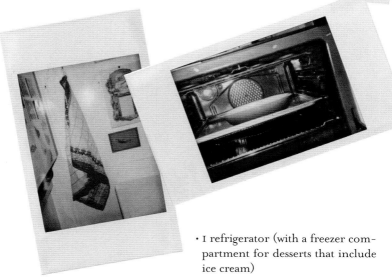

- I refrigerator (with a freezer compartment for desserts that include ice cream)

As you can see, this is all fairly basic equipment. Of course, you won't need every item for every recipe. In some cases, you won't even need a cooktop or oven.

"What about the microwave?" you may exclaim on reading this list.

Well, we've left it out deliberately! Whatever people may say, a microwave is more for reheating things than for actual cooking. And it certainly won't impress the girls. Having said that, when you are preparing accompanying dishes in advance (rice, potatoes...), you can warm them up at the last minute in your microwave, rather than use a saucepan.

How to put together a menu

Generally speaking, a meal consists of an appetizer, a main dish, and a dessert, but you do not have to stick to this pattern too closely.

· You can serve some snacks with the aperitif, and do without the appetizer.
· You can also make your meal consist of a main dish, salad, cheese, and a dessert (after all, the aim is not to end up full to bursting). In this case, it is a good idea to serve the salad and cheese together.
· Since there are only the two of you, you can offer just one cheese. If you don't know her preferences and you don't want to get it wrong, choose two or three different ones. For example, a goat cheese, a hard cheese, and a soft, blue-veined one.

Of course, the aim is to impress, but that does not stop you from buying a ready-made appetizer or dessert. You just need to show you have given it a bit of thought, for example by choosing an authentic local product, a specialty from another country, a cake from a good bakery...

To add value, serve them with a little something extra, for example:
· for cold cuts: an interesting type of bread (incorporating walnuts, raisins, seeds...);
· for tarama, fish roes, smoked salmon: blinis (thick, ready-made pancakes), lemon cut into quarters and fresh cream;
· for a fruit pie: some good quality freshly whipped cream.

Selecting the right recipes

- Calculate how much time you have. Some things can be prepared in advance, saving you time on the evening itself (this is made clear in the individual recipes). Give yourself plenty of time: You won't feel relaxed if your guest rings the doorbell while you are still hard at it in the kitchen.
- Make sure you have the equipment you need. If you have only one saucepan, check that you won't have to use it for the main course and the accompaniment.
- Go for variety. For example, don't plan a tartlet as an appetizerter and a pie as a dessert.
- Choose seasonal dishes (on the whole, it is nicer to eat hot food in winter, cold in summer).

Choosing dishes to match the type of girl

OK, listing girls by type is bound to be a crude oversimplification. It's just to point you in the right direction. You need to use your intuition (you do have some!) in anticipating what she will like and choosing what will melt her heart…

The hipster
Original, modern dishes reflecting the spirit of the age; bold combinations of flavors will show her you are a "with it" sort of guy.

Tomato crumble with Parmesan
Salmon cooked on one side with orange vinaigrette
Apple crunchies with raisins and honey

The weightwatcher
No cream or butter, or very little. You could spoil her evening. Offer her light but tasty dishes she can eat without being overcome by guilt.

Mushroom salad with herbs
Salmon packages with ginger
Orange fruit salad

The fun-loving type
At the table (as elsewhere), enjoyment is her main concern, with no restrictions… so, no criticism, no holding back: You are going to have a ball!

Goat cheese and endive tartlets
Pork tenderloin with Roquefort
Shortbread cookies with banana and hazelnut spread

The society gal

Without going for jugged hare, lobster thermidor, or chicken gumbo (you're not quite ready for those yet), you will please her by choosing more traditional dishes—something with a classical pedigree!

Asparagus with a cream and mustard sauce
Boneless duck breast with a honey and orange sauce
Apple tartlets

The internationalist (a bit of a hippy)

The meal is an opportunity to take her on a trip. Foreign specialties and exotic spices will have the desired effect. Organic products should also touch a sensitive spot.

Zucchini stuffed with feta cheese and mint
Pork fillet, Indonesian style
Apple and date crumble with coconut

The vegetarian

You can automatically cross off all meat, poultry, and fish—anything that was once an animal. But be careful: There are several kinds of vegetarianism. The best thing is to ask her what she cannot eat.

Endive, Swiss cheese, and dried fig salad
Pasta with lemon and parmesan
Strawberries and banana envelopes

Also, if she is Jewish or Muslim, to avoid embarrassment don't serve her pork, whether in the form of ham, bacon, or sausage, or a cut of meat. If you know she practices her religion and you are not familiar with the customs, you'd better discuss it with her, because the rules can be quite complicated.

Going shopping

· Make a list of the things you need, so you don't forget anything.

· Do your shopping the day before or in the morning, to give you a second chance if you can't find everything. You will also be able to prepare some things in advance.

· If you have time and there is one near you, go to a butcher store, a delicatessen, or a fruit and vegetable store, because they will give you useful advice... Don't worry if that's not feasible; you can find plenty of quality products at the supermarket.

· If you don't know much about wine, go to a specialist wine store, tell them how much you are prepared to spend and what the main dish is going to be. They will recommend a wine and tell you a few things you can impress her with during the conversation over dinner.

· When buying bread, go to a bakery: It will be of higher quality.

Where to find things in the supermarket

Here are a few tips for finding your way around the maze of aisles in the supermarket:

- Fruits, vegetables, salad vegetables, and fresh herbs (mint, chives, etc.) are displayed in the same section.

- Spices, salt, pepper, and dried herbs are also generally grouped together.

- You will find poultry, meat, and fish sold already cut up and prepacked in the chilled meat section. Sometimes there is also a meat and fish counter, where the staff will cut and prepare exactly what you need.

- Dairy products (butter, milk, packaged cheese, fresh cream, yogurts, etc.) are displayed together in a refrigerated area. There may also be a cheese counter, offering a wider variety of cheeses.

- There is a special area for prepacked cold cuts, pâté, etc.

- There may be a delicatessen department, and again someone to serve you cold cuts.

- Dry pasta (e.g. spaghetti), rice, and sauces are often displayed together. In the same section, you will find exotic products (soy sauce, coconut milk).

- In the area where sugar is displayed, you will often also find ingredients for cake making (raisins, marzipan, shelled nuts, flaked coconut, etc.).

Getting down to business

· Have paper towels, aluminum foil, and plastic wrap ready to hand, for wiping up, keeping things warm, or wrapping them.

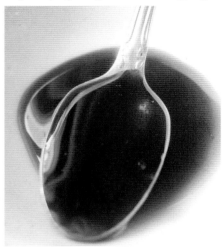

· Not all ovens and stoves heat things in the same way. While cooking, whether you are using a skillet, a saucepan, or the oven, keep a close eye on things. If you see that something is getting too hot (basically, if there is a smell of burning or food is turning too brown), take it off the cooktop and lower the temperature before continuing.

· Above all, read the recipe right through and keep it near you if you want to avoid unpleasant surprises along the way.

· Get out, measure, and prepare all the ingredients and utensils you will need.

· If there is no clock in your kitchen, keep your watch within easy reach to monitor cooking times.

· Always check the "best before" date on the packaging of fresh ingredients.

Setting the table

- A well-set table will score you points. That does not necessarily mean getting out your grandmother's silverware, but pay attention to detail. For example, attractive paper napkins or candles (even the little ones used for warming a hotplate) will create a festive, romantic atmosphere.

- Set out the condiments (salt and pepper), water (in a bottle or carafe), and bread, cut into pieces in a basket or on a small plate.

- Place the knife on the right, the fork on the left, and the plate in the middle... OK, you know that already! Just making sure. Some finer points: Place knives with the cutting edge of the blade toward the plate, and forks with the prongs upward.

- If possible, have two glasses for each place setting: one for wine, one for water.

- Do not set the dessert cutlery (spoon or knife and fork, depending on the food you are serving) until the time comes.

"D"-day, shortly before "H"-hour:
a few tips to make sure the meal goes smoothly

· To make sure the evening unfolds as you have dreamed, without having to abandon your guest every two minutes, some organization is required. You can ask her to keep you company in the kitchen, but being under scrutiny may cause you unnecessary stress.

· Prepare as many things as possible in advance, then all you will have to do is combine the ingredients and cook them.

· Set the table before she arrives, then you'll be more relaxed while enjoying the aperitif.

· If you are planning to serve cheese, take it out of the refrigerator before the beginning of the meal; it has more taste when allowed to "breathe."

· If your main dish takes more than 15 minutes to cook, you can start it when you serve the appetizer. But you may just as well wait until you have finished; no need to hurry over a good meal.

· At the table, it should be you who serves the wine. You can help yourselves to water.

· Change the plates after each course. You can, however, keep the main course plates for the salad and cheese, unless the main course was fish or seafood.

· Since there are just the two of you, you can serve out the accompaniments in the kitchen, before putting the plates on the table. This does away with the need for serving dishes.

Appetizers

Personal experiences

Marie bet she could guess what ingredients I had used. She lost the bet! (Her penalty was our first kiss.)
Christopher, 39, electrical engineer

Sandra was expecting to be served potato chips and peanuts… I got off to a good start!
Thomas (47), lawyer

With the air-dried beef rolls, I had Laura eating out of my hand right from the start.
Julien, 22, department manager

When I told Valerie we were having some pâté, she exclaimed: "Oh no, I've got to look after my figure!" I had anticipated that reaction, but she wolfed down my tuna pâté.
Antoine, 30, French teacher

It was warm and melty… like the atmosphere I wanted to create for Caroline.
Lionel, 35, in advertising

Roquefort butter with raisins

Blending Roquefort cheese with butter gives it a milder taste and the raisins add an original touch of sweetness.

How long it will take

10 minutes

The equipment you need

- 1 bowl
- 1 fork
- 1 spreading knife
Optional:
- 1 tablespoon

Shopping list

- 2 ounces (50) grams of **Roquefort** (work out the amount you need from the weight of the piece you have bought)
- 1/2 stick (50) grams of **butter**
- 1 **French bread** for spreading the mixture on
- 2 handfuls of **raisins**
Optional:
- 2 tablespoons of port

Method

Put the butter and the Roquefort (with the port, if you decide to include it) in the bowl and mash them up with the fork until they are evenly blended. When serving, spread the mixture on slices of French bread and top with a sprinkling of raisins.

Advance preparation

The Roquefort butter can be prepared 2 days in advance. Keep it in the refrigerator, in aluminum foil or plastic wrap.

Panfried ravioli

An original way of serving ravioli with the aperitif.

How long it will take
10 minutes

The equipment you need
- 1 plate
- 1 cooktop
- 1 nonstick skillet
- 1 tablespoon
- 1 fork
- 1 dish or 1 bowl
- 2 sheets of paper towels

Shopping list
- 2 handfuls of **ravioli** (these are the small ravioli stuffed with cheese or other ingredients; you can get them in the supermarket, with the fresh pasta). They can also be bought frozen. You will need 2 handfuls
- 2 tablespoons of **oil**

Method
Spread out the paper towels on a plate. If the ravioli are in linked together, separate them gently along the marked lines. Heat the skillet. When it is hot, pour in the oil. To check that the pan is hot, pass your hand over it (without actually touching, of course) or drip some oil on it: The oil should smoke and evaporate very quickly. When the oil is nice and hot (it should only take 30 seconds), add in the ravioli. Fry them for about 2 minutes on either side, until they are golden brown. Use the tablespoon and the fork to turn them over. This is tricky, because you have to turn them one at a time. Then lay the hot ravioli on the paper towels to absorb the surplus oil. Put them in a dish and serve them immediately, providing forks or teaspoons.

Air-dried beef rolls with figs

A delicious and easy-to-prepare appetizer.

How long it will take
10 minutes

The equipment you need
· 1 sharp knife
· 1 spreading knife

Shopping list
· 6 slices of **air-dried beef** (or bresaola,
  an Italian equivalent)
  (you can get it, vacuum-packed, from the
  cold cuts section of the supermarket or
  from a delicatessen)
· 3 **dried figs**
  (or 1 handful of raisins)
· 1/3 cup (50 grams) of **fromage frais**
  **(in the section with yogurt and cottage
  cheese; substitute whipped cream
  cheese if necessary)**

Method
Remove the stems from the figs and cut them into slices (if you are using raisins, leave them as they are). Cut each slice of air-dried beef in half lengthwise. Spread each half with fromage frais or cream cheese, top this with 1 slice of fig or a few raisins, then roll it all up to form a little "cigar."

Advance preparation
The meat rolls can be prepared the day before. Keep them in the refrigerator, on a plate covered with plastic wrap.

Mini stuffed tomatoes

These appetizers are fresh and attractive-looking, but need delicate handling. Better prepare them one day when you are feeling relaxed.

How long it will take

15 minutes

The equipment you need

- 1 small, sharp knife
- 1 teaspoon
- 1 plate
- 1 bowl
- 1 lemon squeezer

Shopping list

- 12 cherry tomatoes (small but tasty)
- 1/2 lemon + 3 1/2 tablespoons (50 grams) of taramasalata (a Greek spread made with smoked cod roe)
- or 3 1/2 tablespoons (50 grams) of fromage frais (substitute whipped cream cheese if necessary) · or 2 1/2 tablespoons (50 grams) of tapenade (a paste made from olives)

Method

Cut off the top of the tomato at the end where it was attached to the vine. Using the knife and teaspoon, carefully remove the contents (juice and seeds), taking care not to spoil the appearance of the tomato. Place the tomato shells upside down on a plate to drain. Squeeze the half lemon to get the equivalent of 2 tablespoons of juice and pour it into the bowl. If you do not have a lemon squeezer, squeeze it by hand. Remove any pits. Mix the taramasalata in the bowl with the lemon juice. Now fill each tomato with the lemon-flavored taramasalata. Follow the same procedure for the other fillings (cheese or tapenade), but leave out the lemon juice.

Tuna pâté

This can be served with the aperitif or as an appetizer.

How long it will take

10 minutes

The equipment you need

· paper towels
· 1 small knife
· 1 fork
· 1 bowl
Optional:
· 1 lemon squeezer
· 1 pair of scissors for cutting herbs
· 1 toaster

Shopping list

· 1 small **can of tuna** of approximately 6 ounces (170 grams). Buy the kind of can you can pull open without having to use a can opener. Choose tuna in brine for a lighter version of the recipe, tuna in oil for a more creamy result.
· approximately 5 tablespoons (75 grams) of **fromage frais**; for a lighter result, use a low-fat version (substitute whipped cream cheese if necessary)
· sliced bread, wholewheat/country style (or, to be more original, bread containing olives)
· 20 stems of **chives** (or 5 mint leaves or 20 cilantro leaves, or 20 chervil leaves); these herbs will give the pâté a fresh taste and an attractive appearance
· 1/2 **lemon**

Method

Wash the herbs and dry them with paper towels. Cut them into tiny pieces with the knife or scissors. Drain the tuna by opening the can lid slightly and letting the liquid drip into the sink. Squeeze the 1/2 lemon and pour the juice into the bowl. If you do not have a lemon squeezer, squeeze it by hand. Remove any pits. Put all the ingredients in the bowl (except for 1 large spoonful of cut herbs) and mash

with a fork until you have achieved an even consistency. Scatter the herbs you have set aside on the pâté to make it look nice. If you have a toaster, toast the slices of bread.

Advance preparation
The pâté can be prepared 2 days in advance. Keep it in the refrigerator, covered.

Starters

Personal experiences

Melanie couldn't believe I had done it myself. I had to go through the recipe stage-by-stage to convince her.
Freddy, 19, student

Mamma mia, Italian food is a big hit with women! Ask Elinor…
Paolo, 25, stage director

Apart from heating up frozen dinners, Geraldine hasn't a clue about cooking. I've become her hero.
Nicolas, 27, accountant

"Your place is better than a restaurant; you really are a man of surprises!" And that was not the last compliment Louise paid me that evening.

Michael, 41, writer

Sweet-and-sour, that sums up Nathalie. But that evening she liked the meal I had prepared so much, she was all honey...

Steven, 32, salesman

Angela is half English, so she thought she knew a thing or two about making a crumble. I was really able to call her bluff.

Emmanuel, 28, IT specialist

Tomato crumble with Parmesan

As a change from apple crumble, try this tomato-based version.

How long it takes

20 minutes for the preparation
+ 25 minutes' cooking time

The equipment you need

· 1 oven
· 1 small, sharp knife
· 1 ovenproof dish (for 2 persons)
· 1 teaspoon
· 1 tablespoon
· 1 measuring cup
· 1 bowl for preparing the crumble

Shopping list

· 4 **tomatoes**
· 1/4 cup (about 50 grams) of grated **Parmesan**
· 5 or 6 leaves of **basil** (optional)
· 1 teaspoon of **oil**
· 2 tablespoons of **balsamic vinegar** (a specialty vinegar you will find on the oil and vinegar shelf in the supermarket)
· 1/2 stick (50 grams) of **butter**
· 1/4 cup of **all-pupose flour**
· 1/2 teaspoon of **salt**

Method

Set the oven to 180 °F. It takes 20 minutes for an electric oven to heat up, 10 minutes for a gas oven (some ovens have a light which goes off when the desired temperature has been reached). Rinse and dry the tomatoes. Cut them into quarters, then cut each quarter in half and remove the seeds with the knife or a spoon. Cut each piece of tomato into small dice. Spread the oil on the bottom of the ovenproof dish and add the pieces of tomato. Sprinkle with salt and pour on the balsamic vinegar. Stir. Wash and dry the basil leaves, if you have some (but keep two for decoration), cut them into strips, and spread them over the tomatoes.

If the dish is rather big for the quantity of tomatoes, push them together on one side of the dish and leave part of it empty. Cut the butter into small pieces. Place the butter, the flour, and the Parmesan in the bowl. Knead the ingredients with your fingers, making sure you break down the pieces of butter until the flour and Parmesan are fully blended in. The resulting mixture should be fairly grainy. Spread this mixture over the tomatoes to form a crust. Put the dish in the oven and leave it to cook about 25 minutes by which time the crust should be a golden color. Take a look occasionally to make sure it is not getting too brown. If it is, lower the temperature to 150 °F and let it continue to cook. If, on the other hand, the crust is not golden after 20 minutes, increase the temperature to 210 °F. When it is done, remove the dish from the oven using an oven glove. Leave it to cool 5 minutes, then put a basil leaf on top.

Advance preparation
The day before, you can cut up the tomatoes (without seasoning them) and prepare the butter–flour–Parmesan mixture. Keep them separately in the refrigerator in aluminum foil or plastic wrap.

Goat cheese and endive tartlets

This is quite a substantial appetizer. Honey is included to take away the bitterness of the endives.

How long it will take

10 minutes for preparation
+ 20 minutes' frying time in the pan
+ 12 to 15 minutes' cooking time in the oven

The equipment you need

· 1 oven
· 1 knife
· 1 cooktop
· baking parchment roll or sheet
· 1 bottle
· 1 nonstick skillet or 1 saucepan
· 1 baking tray
· 1 spatula
· 1 small bowl
· 1 fork
· 1 teaspoon

Shopping list

· 1 package of ready-to-bake frozen **puff pastry**
· 4 **endives**
· 2 small round **goat cheeses**; you will need around 5 ounces (140 grams)
· 1 knob of **butter**
· 1 teaspoon of **honey** (or 1 teaspoon of sugar)
· 1 pinch of **salt**

Method

Defrost the package of puff pastry in the microwave to allow it to soften and make it easier to unroll (or remove from the refrigerator if you have placed it there the day before). Take out the baking tray on which the tartlets are to be cooked and line it with baking parchment. Set the oven to 400 °F. It takes 20 minutes for an electric oven to heat up, 10 minutes for a gas oven (some ovens have an indicator

44

light which goes off when the desired temperature has been reached). Cut off the end bit at the base of the endives and remove any spoiled outer leaves (you do not need to wash the endives). Then cut them into slices 2/3 inch (2 centimeters) long.

Heat the butter in the skillet or saucepan, over a low flame. When it has melted, add the

endives, the salt, and the honey. Let these ingredients cook for 20 minutes, stirring occasionally, until the endives are transparent and soft. They will lose water and shrink during the cooking process. Cut the goat cheeses into slices roughly 1/8 inch (3 millimeters) thick. Roll out the pastry, using the bottle as a rolling pin. Place the small bowl rim down on the pastry, very near the edge, and press hard to cut out a circular piece. If it does not come away cleanly, cut it out with a knife. Repeat this step for the second tartlet. Remove the excess dough. Spread half of the cooked endive leaves on each circle of pastry, covering them completely. Then top with the slices of cheese. When the oven is heated up, place the tartlets on the lined baking tray and put them in the oven on the middle shelf. Cook 12 to 15 minutes. If the pastry begins to brown too much, lower the temperature to 350 °F. The tartlets are ready when the goat cheese is melted and golden. Remove the tartlets from the oven and slide them onto the plates using a fork. They are ready to eat.

Advance preparation
If you don't have a microwave, place the puff pastry dough in the refrigerator the day before to defrost. The endives can be cooked the day before.

Breaded goat cheese with hazelnuts

An original version of a French classic.

How long it will take

15 minutes + 5 minutes' cooking time

The equipment you need

- 1 plate
- 1 small bowl
- 1 fork
- 1 salad bowl
- 1 cooktop
- 1 nonstick skillet
- 1 spatula
- 1 tablespoon
- 1 small, sharp knife
Optional:
- 1 bottle
- paper towels

Shopping list

- 2 small round **goat cheeses** (a little on the dry side)
- 8 tablespoons of **hazelnut flour** (you can find it on the baking ingredients shelf in the supermarket) or 8 tablespoons of **dried breadcrumbs** (you can buy them ready for use) or 4 rusks
- 1 **egg**
- 2 handfuls of **lettuce** (you can buy it ready to use in a bag)
- 5 tablespoons of **oil** (2 to cook the goat cheeses and 3 for the salad)
- 1 tablespoon of **vinegar**
Optional:
- 2 shelled **hazelnuts**, for decoration

Method

Pour the hazelnut flour or breadcrumbs out onto the plate. If using rusks, crush them to obtain a fairly fine powder. The easiest way is to use a bottle. Break the egg into the small bowl and beat it with the fork to blend the yolk and the egg white. Cut the goat cheeses in half horizontally to obtain 4 round halves. Wash and dry the lettuce, unless you bought it ready to use in a bag. Place it in the salad bowl. Pour 3 large tablespoons of oil over it.

Turn the salad, so that the lettuce leaves are well covered in oil, then add the vinegar and turn again. Get the plates out and put half of the salad on each. Using your fingers, dip each half goat cheese in the beaten egg, making sure they are covered in egg, then dip them in the hazelnut flour (or breadcrumbs, or crushed rusks), turning then to make sure the whole surface is covered. Heat the skillet over a medium flame. When it is hot, pour in the oil. To check whether the skillet is hot, pass your hand over it (without actually touching it, of course) or drip a few drops of water onto it; it should hiss and evaporate quickly. When the oil is hot (it takes only about 30 seconds), place the half goat cheeses in the pan. Fry them for about 2 minutes on each side, until they are a golden color, turning them over gently with the spatula, with the help of a tablespoon if necessary. Place 2 breaded half goat cheeses on each plate on top of the salad. Sprinkle with a little of the remaining hazelnut flour or decorate with a hazelnut.

Asparagus with a cream and mustard sauce

The asparagus season runs from April to June. This sauce makes a change from lemon and butter.

How long it will take

15 minutes' preparation
+ 15 to 25 minutes' cooking time

The equipment you need

- 1 cooktop
- 1 large saucepan
- 1 knife
- 1 tablespoon
- 1 teaspoon
- 1 potato peeler
- 1 dish or 1 plate
- 1 small bowl
- 2 forks
- some sheets of paper towels or 1 clean dish towel

Optional:

- 1 microwave oven

Shopping list

- **asparagus: roughly 8 stalks if they are very thick (more than 2/3 inch (2 centimeters) in diameter), 12 if they are thin (less than 1/3 inch (1 centimeter) in diameter), 10 if they are somewhere in between; they should weigh between 1 and 1 1/3 pounds (500 and 600 grams)**
- 3 tablespoons of **heavy cream**
- 2 teaspoons of **mustard** (for extra effect, use some wholegrain mustard: the grains look attractive in the sauce)
- 1/2 teaspoon of **paprika** (a red spice in powder form, sold in a small jar)
- **salt**

Method

Boil some water in a saucepan with 1 tablespoon of salt. Cut a small bit off the bottom of the asparagus stalks. Peel the stalks with the potato peeler, beginning just below the tip (the tender, pointed end of the asparagus) and continuing downward.

Be careful not to damage the tips. When the water is boiling hard, put in the asparagus and let them cook between 15 and 25 minutes, depending on their thickness. Meanwhile, mix the cream, the mustard, and 1/3 teaspoon of salt in the

bowl. Place the dish towel or 3 paper towels on a plate. To check that the asparagus is cooked, prick one of the stalks with the point of the knife; it should go in easily. Carefully lift them from the saucepan using 2 forks and place them on the plate. Wait 5 minutes for them to drain and cool down before serving. Put half of the asparagus on each plate, pour half of the sauce beside them and sprinkle with papri-

ka. It looks nicer if you spread out the asparagus in a single, even layer.

Advance preparation

The sauce can be prepared the day before. Before your guest arrives, you can cook the asparagus and leave them to drain on the paper towels. They can be eaten warm or cold. To reheat them, the best way is to put them in the microwave for a few minutes.

Cucumbers with a cream and herb sauce

Cucumbers are at their best in the spring and summer. This cool, light appetizer is very simple to prepare.

How long it will take

10 minutes

The equipment you need

- 1 knife
- 1 clean dish towel or some paper towels
- 1 potato peeler
- 1 tablespoon
- 1 teaspoon
- 1 salad bowl

Optional:

- 1 pair of scissors

Shopping list

- ½ **cucumber**
- 2 tablespoons of **heavy cream**
- 20 stems of **chives** or 8 mint leaves, or 12 cilantro leaves, or 12 leaves of chervil
- 1/2 teaspoon of **salt**

Method

Wash and dry the herbs. Cut them into small pieces with the knife or a pair of scissors. Peel the cucumber with the potato peeler. Cut it into slices roughly 2/3 inch (2 millimeters) thick. Put all the ingredients in the salad bowl and mix them.

Crunchy envelopes of goat cheese and olives

The phyllo dough and olives give this appetizer a Mediterranean feel.

How long it will take

15 minutes' preparation
+ 6 minutes' cooking time

The equipment you need

- 1 knife
- 2 plates
- 1 salad bowl
- 1 tablespoon
- 1 cooktop
- 1 nonstick skillet
- 1 spatula

Shopping list

- 2 **sheets of frozen phyllo dough** (very thin sheets of dough, which you will find in the supermarket, or in Oriental or Middle Eastern grocery stores; they come in packs containing several sheets)
- 2 small round **goat cheeses** (you need roughly 4 ounces (120 grams))
- 10 or so pitted **olives** (green or black)
- 2 handfuls of **lettuce** leaves (you can buy them ready washed in a bag)
- 5 tablespoons of **oil** (2 for cooking the phyllo pastry envelopes and 3 for the salad)
- 1 tablespoon of **vinegar**

Method

Defrost the package of phyllo dough in the microwave to allow it to soften (or remove from the refrigerator if you have placed it there the day before). Cut the olives in half. Cut each goat cheese horizontally into 4 slices. Remove the sheets of phyllo dough from their packaging. They are separated by sheets of paper to prevent them from sticking together. Take one of them, very carefully because they are fragile, and lay it on a plate. Place one of the goat cheeses cut into 4 pieces and half of the olives in the middle of the dough square. Fold in the edges of the dough to form a square envelope.

Repeat the operation with the second phyllo sheet. Wash and dry the lettuce, unless it is ready washed in the bag. Place it in the salad bowl. Pour 3 tablespoons of oil over it and turn well, making sure that the leaves are coated in oil, then add the vinegar, and turn again. Get out the plates and put half of the salad on each. Heat the remainder of the oil in the skillet over a medium flame and gently place the 2 phyllo pastry envelopes in the pan, folded side down. Let them cook 2 to 3 minutes. The dough will become crunchy and golden. Turn the envelopes over gently using the spatula, and let them cook a further 2 minutes. If the oil is too hot and the pastry squares begin to become too brown, lower the heat. Cut each envelope in half to form 2 triangles, and place them on the salad. The meal is ready.

Bruschetta with tomato

An Italian appetizer, best in summer, when tomatoes are more flavorsome.

How long it will take

20 minutes

The equipment you need

- 1 sharp knife
- 1 tablespoon
- 1 bowl
- 1 toaster or 1 oven
- 1 clean dish towel or some paper towels

Shopping list

- 2 ripe **tomatoes**
- 4 tablespoons of **olive oil**
- 1/2 clove of **garlic**
- 12 stalks of fresh **basil** (otherwise, use some ready-cut frozen basil; you will need roughly 3 tablespoons)
- 2 large or 4 small slices of **bakery white bread**
- **salt** and **pepper**

Method

Rinse the tomatoes in cold water, then dry them with a dish towel or some paper towels. Cut them in quarters, then cut each quarter in half and remove the seeds with the knife or a spoon. Cut each slice of tomato into 4 or 5 more pieces. Put them in the bowl. Wash and dry the basil leaves (set 2 or 4 aside for decorative purposes). Cut them into thin strips and spread them over the tomatoes. Pour 2 tablespoons of oil on top and mix the contents of the bowl. Peel the 1/2 clove of garlic (remove the dry skin). Toast the slices of bread in the toaster or put under the broiler (in this case, you will have to turn them over so that they are toasted on both sides). When the slices of bread are toasted brown, rub them on one side with the garlic, then pour the remainder of the oil over them. Place the bread on the plates and spread the diced tomato on top. Season to taste.

Mushroom salad with herbs

A light, very tasty starter, thanks to the mixture of herbs and Swiss cheese.

How long it will take

15 minutes

The equipment you need

- 1 knife
- 1 potato peeler
- 1 tablespoon
- 1 bowl
- 1 measuring cup
- 1 clean dish towel or some paper towels

Optional:
- 1 pair of scissors for cutting up the herbs

Shopping list

- 1 cup (100 grams) of **fresh mushrooms**
- 8 stems of **chives**
- 5 **basil** leaves
- 5 **mint** leaves
- 2 ounces Swiss cheese (40 to 50 grams)
- 4 tablespoons of **oil** (olive, walnut, or canola)
- 1 tablespoon of **vinegar** (balsamic, sherry, or wine)
- **salt** and **pepper**

Method

Wash and dry the herbs (if you cannot find them all, use any of fresh chervil, parsley, cilantro, or tarragon: The important thing is to have a good mix). Keep a few leaves uncut for decoration. Cut the others into small pieces with the knife or scissors. Quickly rinse the mushrooms in cold water to remove any dirt, but do not let them soak up any water. Dry them immediately. Cut the end off the stalk of each mushroom, then cut them as thinly as possible, vertically, from the cap to the base.

Use the potato peeler to cut the cheese into slivers. Pour the oil and vinegar into the bowl, then mix them. Add the mushrooms, herbs, and cheese. Mix the salad.

Season with salt and pepper. Decorate with the herbs you set aside. It is ready to serve.

Advance preparation
This salad can be prepared earlier in the evening before your guest arrives.

Blue cheese and pear tartlets

The sugary taste of the pear is a perfect match for the saltiness of the blue cheese.

How long it will take

20 minutes' preparation
+ 15 minutes' cooking time

The equipment you need

- 1 oven
baking parchment
- bottle
- 1 knife
- 1 potato peeler
- 1 small bowl
- 1 tablespoon
- 1 fork
- 1 lemon squeezer

Shopping list

- 1 package of ready-to-bake frozen **puff pastry** dough
- 1/2 **pear**
- 1/2 **lemon**
- roughly 4 ounces (115 grams) of **blue cheese**; estimate the amount from the weight information on the packaging

Method

Defrost the package of puff pastry in the microwave to allow it to soften and make it easier to roll out (or remove from the refrigerator if you have placed it there the day before). Remove from the oven the baking tray or broiler pan on which you are going to cook the tartlets and line with baking parchment. Heat the oven to 400 °F. It takes 20 minutes for an electric oven to heat up, 10 minutes for a gas oven (some ovens have an indicator light to show when the desired temperature has been reached). Cut the 1/2 pear into 2 quarters. Slice one thin layer of pear from each quarter with the potato peeler (to use for decoration), then peel them and remove the core. Cut them into thin slices. Squeeze the 1/2 lemon and pour the juice into the bowl. Pour the equivalent of 1 tablespoon of juice over the slices of pear to prevent them from oxidizing (and going brown).

Cut the cheese into slices about 1/8 inch (3 millimeters) thick. Roll out the dough using the bottle as a rolling pin. Wash and dry the small bowl and place it rim down on the dough, very near the edge. Press down hard to cut out a circular piece. If it does not come away cleanly, cut it out with a knife. Repeat this step for the second tartlet. Remove the excess dough. When the oven is heated, place the tartlets on the lined baking tray or broiler pan and put them in the oven. Leave them to cook 5 minutes, then remove the baking tray or broiler pan from the oven and place it on a heat-resistant surface or table mat. If the puff pastry has swollen up, press down lightly to flatten it again. Place the slices of pear on the circles of pastry and return them to the oven a further 5 minutes. Next, remove the baking tray or broiler pan again and place the thin slices of cheese on top of the pears. Return to the oven a further 5 minutes. The cheese should then be nicely melted. Remove the tartlets from the oven and slide them onto the plates using a fork. Decorate with the slices of pear you set aside earlier.

Advance preparation

Earlier in the evening, before your guest arrives, cook the puff pastry, first on its own, then with the pears. Then all you need to do when she arrives is add the cheese and cook 5 minutes.

Zucchini stuffed with feta cheese and mint

An appetizer with a Greek flavor. Double the quantities and it can be presented as a vegetarian main course.

How long it will take

25 minutes' preparation
+ 30 minutes' cooking time

The equipment you need

- 1 ovenproof dish (or 1 baking tray or 1 broiler pan + some aluminum foil
- 1 oven
- 1 clean dish towel or some paper towels
- 1 knife
- 1 teaspoon
- 1 tablespoon
- 1 small bowl
- 1 fork

Optional:
- 1 pair of scissors for cutting up the herbs

Shopping list

- 1 **zucchini**
- 6 **mint** leaves
- 4 ounces (115) grams of **feta cheese** (a sheep cheese of Greek origin, usually sold in 8 ounce packs)
- 2 tablespoons of **olive oil**

Method

Get out the ovenproof dish (or the baking tray or broiler pan on which you are going to cook the zucchini halves). Set the oven to 350 °F. It takes 20 minutes for an electric oven to heat up, 10 minutes for a gas oven (some ovens have an indicator light to show when the desired temperature has been reached). Wash the zucchini and dry it with a dish towel. Cut it in half lengthwise. Use a small spoon to gently dig the seeds from each half to make room for the stuffing. Wash and dry the mint

leaves, then cut them into thin strips (keeping two aside for decoration).
Put the feta cheese, the mint, and the oil in the bowl. Crush them with the fork
and mix them together. Using the teaspoon, fill the zucchini halves with this mixture, pressing it down well. Place the zucchini halves on some aluminum foil in
the ovenproof dish (or on the baking tray or broiler pan,) and cook 30 minutes
in the oven. When they are ready, place one stuffed zucchini half on each plate,
decorate with a mint leaf, and serve.

Layered goat cheese and cucumber with raisins

A tasty, refreshing and original appetizer.

How long it will take

20 minutes

The equipment you need

- 1 tablespoon
- 1 small bowl
- 1 knife
- 1 potato peeler

Optional:

- 1 lemon squeezer

Shopping list

- ½ **cucumber** (unless it is a small one, in which case use it all)
- ½ **lemon**
- 3 tablespoons of **olive oil**
- 2 small round goat cheeses, slightly on the dry side (you will need 4 ounces (between 100 and 120 grams))
- 1 handful of **raisins**
- **salt** and **pepper**

Method

Squeeze the lemon to obtain the equivalent of 1 tablespoon of juice, and pour it into the bowl. If you do not have a lemon squeezer, squeeze it by hand. Remove any pits. Pour the oil into the bowl. Add a pinch of salt, a pinch of pepper, and mix. Cut off both ends of the cucumber. Peel it with the potato peeler and cut it into slices about 1/8 inch (3 millimeters) thick. Cut the goat cheeses into slices, also about 1/8 inch (3 millimeters) thick. On each plate, place 2 slices of cucumber, then 2 slices of cheese on top of them. Continue in this way, finishing off each creation with a piece of cucumber. Sprinkle with raisins. Pour on the lemon dressing, and they are ready to serve.

Endive, Swiss cheese, and dried fig salad

This salad can be served as an appetizer, or you can omit the appetizer and serve it between the main dish and the dessert.

How long it will take

15 minutes

The equipment you need

· 1 small sharp knife
· 1 salad bowl
· 1 teaspoon
· 1 tablespoon
· 1 potato peeler
· 1 measuring cup

Shopping list

· 4 **endives**
· 4 **dried figs** (or 1 handful of raisins)
· 1 teaspoon of **mustard** (wholegrain or Dijon)
· 1 tablespoon of **vinegar**
· 3 tablespoons of **oil**
· roughly 4 ounces (115 grams) of **Swiss cheese** (4 ounces [110] grams is roughly the quantity needed to make 1 cup when it has been grated)
· **salt** and **pepper**

Method

Remove the stems from the figs and cut them into thin slices (if you are using raisins, leave them as they are). In the salad bowl, mix the mustard, the vinegar, and the salt, using a spoon. Add 1 tablespoon of oil, and mix again until the ingredients are smoothly blended. Do the same with the remaining 2 spoonfuls of oil. Finally, mix in a pinch of pepper. Slice the Swiss cheese with the potato peeler to produce slivers of cheese. Cut the end from the base of the endives and remove any damaged outer leaves (it is not necessary to wash the endives). Cut the remainder into circles about 1/3 inch (1 centimeter) thick. Just before serving, put the endives and the pieces of fig and Swiss cheese into the salad bowl and mix.

Advance preparation
You can slice the figs and prepare the dressing the day before.

Mozzarella fritters on arugula salad

A delicious and original way to serve mozzarella.

How long it will take

15 minutes + 5 minutes' cooking time

The equipment you need

· I plate
· I bottle
· I small bowl
· I fork
· measuring cup
· I small knife
· I clean dish towel or some paper towels
· I salad bowl
· I nonstick skillet
· I spatula
· I tablespoon
· I cooktop

Shopping list

· I **mozzarella di buffala cheese (made from the milk of the female buffalo it has more taste, or you can buy ordinary mozzarella)**
· ½ cup of **breadcrumbs** (buy them ready-made), or 4 rusks, or 10 grissini (crispy Italian bread sticks to serve with the aperitif)
· I **egg**
· 2 handfuls of **arugula** (a salad vegetable with a distinctive bitter taste) or another type of salad
· 5 tablespoons of **olive oil** (2 for cooking with and 3 for the salad)
· I tablespoon of **balsamic vinegar** (a very mild vinegar you will find on the oil and vinegar shelf at the supermarket)

Method

Pour the breadcrumbs onto a plate, or crush the rusks or grissini to obtain a fairly fine powder. The simplest way to do it is by using a bottle as rolling pin. Break the egg into the small bowl and beat it with a fork to blend the yolk and white. Cut the round mozzarella cheese into 4 slices. Wash and dry the salad, unless it is ready washed in a bag. Put it in the salad bowl.

Pour 3 tablespoons of oil over it. Mix the salad thoroughly, so that the leaves are well covered in oil, then add the vinegar and mix again. Put half of the salad on each plate. Using your fingers, dip each slice of mozzarella in the beaten egg, making sure they are completely coated, then lay them in the breadcrumbs, turning them to make sure the whole surface is covered. Leave them on the plate with the breadcrumbs. Heat the skillet to a high temperature. When it is hot, pour in the remainder of the oil.

To check whether the skillet is hot, pass your hand over it (without actually touching it, of course) or drip a few drops of water onto it; it should smoke and evaporate fairly quickly. When the oil is hot (it takes only about 30 seconds), place the slices of mozzarella in the pan. Fry them about 1 minute on either side until they are a golden color. Turn them over gently with the spatula with the help of the tablespoon, if necessary. Place the mozzarella fritters on the arugula leaves and serve.

Main dishes

Personal experiences

If someone had told me that one day I would be cooking sole meunière, and that a girl as pretty as Julie would be asking for a second helping, I would never have believed it.

Thomas, 41, administrator

When I casually asked Helen to come and have some pasta, I think she was expecting frozen ravioli…

John, 20, actor

Since Angie is something of a traditionalist, I told her it was one of my grandmother's recipes that she had given to no one but me.

Bruno, 45 years old, engineer

Marian admitted to me: Frankly, your Beef Stroganov is better than my mother makes, but if you meet her one day you must promise me you will not tell her I said so.
Vincent (30), photographer

My relationship with Della really took off thanks to this first culinary adventure…
Ralph, 25, salesman

After the meal, Laura was somewhat excited. The effect of the ginger, or my native charm?
Ben (22), student

To seduce a woman, they say you have to make her laugh. I say you have to make her lamb chops with yogurt and mint!
Lionel, 31 years old, plumber

Chicken breasts with paprika sauce

This dish goes well with boiled rice (see p. 112), slow-fried zucchini (see p. 122), or a green salad (see p. 110).

How long it will take

10 minutes' preparation the day before or earlier in the day
+ 15 minutes' preparation and cooking time in the evening

The equipment you need

- 1 small bowl
- 1 tablespoon
- 1 teaspoon
- 1 dish or 1 plate
- 1 cooktop
- 1 nonstick skillet
- 1 spatula
- 1 lemon squeezer
- paper towels

Shopping list

- 2 **chicken breasts** (the white meat)
- ½ **lemon**
- 2 small cartons of **yogurt** (Greek style); for a lighter version of the recipe, choose yogurt containing 0 % fat
- 1 teaspoon of **mustard** (Dijon or wholegrain)
- ½ teaspoon of **paprika** (a red spice in powder form)
- 10 **cilantro** leaves (a highly aromatic green herb), or 6 stems of chives, or 10 chervil leaves, or 4 mint leaves
- 1 tablespoon of **oil**
- **salt** and **pepper**

Method

The day before or earlier in the day, squeeze the ½ lemon and pour the juice into a bowl. If you do not have a lemon squeezer, squeeze it by hand. Remove any pits. Add the yogurt, the mustard, and the paprika, and mix them together with the tablespoon. Add salt and pepper to the mixture, tasting occasionally to make sure you do not overseason it.

Remove the skin from the chicken breasts if it has not already been removed (use your fingers). Place them on the dish or plate and tip half of the yogurt mixture over them. Turn them over so that both sides are coated. Put the dish containing the chicken in the refrigerator, together with the bowl containing the remainder of the sauce, having covered them with aluminum foil or plastic wrap. Leaving the chicken to marinate in the yogurt sauce will make it more tender and flavorsome. **On the evening of the meal, remove the chicken and sauce from the refrigerator. Wipe the chicken breasts. Prepare the cilantro leaves by plucking them from their stalks. Rinse and dry them. Heat the skillet over a high flame. When it is hot, pour in the oil.** To check whether the skillet is hot, pass your hand over it (without actually touching it, of course) or drip a few drops of water onto it; it should smoke and evaporate fairly quickly. When the oil is hot (it takes only about 30 seconds), place the chicken breasts in the pan. Fry them for about 4 minutes on each side. They should be a golden color on the outside, and the flesh inside should be completely white. To check that they are well done, cut into the chicken breast with a small knife.

If it is still underdone, continue cooking. When ready, place the chicken breasts on the plates. Put half of the remaining yogurt sauce on each plate beside the chicken, and decorate each chicken breast with the cilantro leaves (or other herbs) and a little paprika. The meal is ready!

Scallops with pastis

Pastis (an aniseed liqueur) gives the sauce a slight licorice flavor, but does not taste of alcohol. Fresh scallops are available from October to May, but you can get frozen ones at any time of year.

How long it will take

5 minutes' preparation
+ 15 minutes' cooking time

The equipment you need

· I salad bowl (for the frozen scallops)
· I small knife
· I cooktop
· I saucepan
· I nonstick skillet
· I spatula
· I measuring cup
· I tablespoon
· paper towels

Shopping list

· 10 **scallops** without the coral (the pink roe). If you buy them fresh from a fish store, ask them to prepare them for you (if he leaves the coral, remove it yourself with a knife); you can also buy them frozen.
· 4 **leeks**
· ½ cup (50 centiliters) of **milk** (only if your scallops are frozen)
· I knob of **butter**
· ½ cup of **light cream**
· 2 tablespoons of **pastis**
· I tablespoon of **oil**
· **salt** and **pepper**

Method

The day before, if you have bought frozen scallops, remove them from the freezer. Put them in a salad bowl, pour the milk over them, and leave them in a cool place.

On the evening, remove the scallops from the milk, sponge them off with paper towels, and sprinkle salt on both sides. Cut off the dark green sections of the leeks.

Cut off the stringy bulb end. Split the leeks in half lengthwise. Remove the outer layer, then wash them in cold water to remove any dirt. Cut them into sections roughly 1/3 inch (1 centimeter) long. Melt the knob of butter in a saucepan over a low flame, then add the leeks. Season with salt and pepper. Let them cook 15 minutes, stirring from time to time. They will become soft and transparent.

Meanwhile, get out the plates, the light cream and the bottle of pastis. Five minutes before the leeks are done, heat the skillet over a high flame. **When it is hot, pour in the oil.** To check whether the skillet is hot, pass your hand over it (without actually touching it, of course) or drip a few drops of water onto it; it should smoke and evaporate fairly quickly. When the oil is hot (it takes only about 30 seconds), place the scallops in the pan. Turn them over after 1 minute using a spatula. They should be a nice golden color. After a further minute's cooking, pour on the pastis. Lower the temperature and pour on the light cream. Add salt and pepper and leave the scallops to cook another 3 minutes, turning them over once more in the process. The light cream should be

boiling at this point. It will reduce and thicken. Put the scallops on the plates with the sauce and the leeks. Serve immediately.

Beef Stroganov

This simplified version of Beef Stroganov retains the spirit of the traditional recipe. It can be served with fresh pasta (see p. 114) or rice (see p. 112), but neither is essential because the mushrooms and onions are sufficient accompaniment.

How long it will take

20 minutes' preparation
+ 26 minutes' cooking time

The equipment you need

· 1 sharp knife
· 1 tablespoon
· 1 nonstick skillet
· 1 cooktop
· 1 small bowl
· 1 plate
· 1 measuring cup
Optional:
· some aluminum foil or plastic wrap

Shopping list

· ¾ pound (340 grams) of **filet mignon (or use strip steak)**
· 1 **onion**
· 1 can of sliced **mushrooms** weighing about 7 ounces (200 grams) (about 4 ounces (110 grams) when drained); buy a pull-open type of can so you do not need a can opener
· 2 tablespoons of **oil**
· 2 knobs of **butter**
· ½ **lemon**
· 1 tablespoon of **tomato paste**
· 1 teaspoon of **Dijon mustard**
· 4 ounces (12 centiliters) **light cream**
· **salt** and **pepper**

Method

Before your guest arrives, peel the onion, removing the dry outer layers of skin. Cut it in half. Lay the halves flat side down and cut each half into slices about 1/8 inch (1/2 centimeter) thick. Drain the mushrooms by making an opening in the can and pouring the liquid into the sink.

Melt 1 tablespoon of oil and 1 knob of butter in the skillet over a low flame. When the butter has melted, add the slices of onion and leave them to cook 15 minutes. After 15 minutes, add the mushrooms and cook a further 5 minutes. While they are cooking, squeeze the 1/2 lemon to obtain the equivalent of 1 tablespoon of juice and pour it into the bowl. Remove any pits. Add the tomato paste, Dijon mustard, salt, and pepper, and mix them together. Cut the meat into pieces the size of your little finger. When the onion and mushrooms are done, remove them from the pan and set them aside on a plate. No need to wash the skillet.

When the time comes to serve the dish, add half a cup of light cream to the measuring cup. Get the plates out. Put the rest of the oil and butter to melt in the pan over a low flame. When the butter is melted, add the pieces of beef and cook for about 2 minutes; they should be very brown on the outside. Then add in the onions and mushrooms, together with the lemon-tomato-Dijon mustard mixture and cook 2 minutes. Next add the cream and cook a further 2 minutes. Put half of the resulting mixture on each plate and serve.

Jumbo shrimp with a coconut milk and curry sauce

A very light dish with an exotic flavor, best served with basmati rice (see p. 112)

How long it will take

15 minutes' preparation
+ 7 minutes' cooking time

The equipment you need

· I small bowl
· paper towels
· I tablespoon
· I nonstick skillet or I saucepan
· I cooktop
· I measuring cup
· I teaspoon
· I lemon squeezer
Optional:
· I salad bowl
· I can opener, if the coconut milk comes
  in a can

Shopping list

· roughly 3/4 cup (350 grams) of cooked
  shrimp (between 16 and 20 shrimp);
  even with frozen shrimp, the results are
  more than satisfactory
· ½ **lime** (if possible; otherwise use
  a lemon)
· ½ cup of **coconut milk** (you will find
  this in the exotic products department of
  the supermarket, sold in small cardboard
  cartons or cans, or in an Oriental grocery store
· I teaspoon of **curry** powder (a very aromatic mixture of Indian spices, displayed
  with the other spices and condiments)
· roughly 15 **cilantro leaves (a highly
  aromatic green herb)**, or 10 stems of
  chives, or 15 chervil leaves

Method

**The day before, if the shrimps are frozen, remove them from the freezer and
put them in a salad bowl in the refrigerator. Alternatively, read the instructions on the packaging for unfreezing them quickly on the evening of the meal.**

On the evening of the meal, if not already peeled,carefully peel the shrimp using your fingers, removing the head and tail, and the shell. Squeeze the 1/2 lime and pour the juice into a bowl. If you do not have a squeezer, do it by hand. Set aside the equivalent of 1 tablespoon of juice. Add the coconut milk and curry powder, and mix well. Prepare the cilantro leaves by plucking them from their stalks. Rinse and dry them. Pour the sauce into the skillet or saucepan. Heat it over a high flame. When the sauce is boiling (producing large bubbles), lower the temperature and add in the shrimp. Let them cook about 6 minutes. The sauce should bubble slightly. Get out the plates and put half of the shrimp on each. Top them with the sauce and decorate with the coriander leaves.

Advance preparation

You can prepare the sauce the day before and peel the shrimp (unless they are frozen). Keep them in the refrigerator.

Salmon cooked on one side with orange vinaigrette

This style of cooking is simple and delicious: The salmon is crunchy on one side, creamy on the other. The orange vinaigrette is light and aromatic. Serve this dish with rice (see p. 112) or slow-fried zucchini (see p. 122).

How long it will take

10 minutes' preparation
+ 10 minutes' cooking time

The equipment you need

· 1 clean dish towel or some paper towels
· 1 knife
· 1 potato peeler
· 1 small bowl
· 1 cooktop
· 1 tablespoon
· 1 nonstick skillet
· 1 spatula
Optional:
· 1 lemon squeezer
· 1 pair of scissors

Shopping list

· 2 **salmon fillets** weighing about
  5 ounces (150 grams) each, with the skin
  removed. Buy the salmon from a fish
  store or the fish counter of the supermarket, so you can ask the staff to
  remove the skin, which is a tricky
  operation. The highest quality salmon
  is the wild variety (not farmed); this is
  more expensive but well worth it.
· 10 stems of **chives** (or 3 tablespoons
  of frozen chives, which will be cut up
  already)
· 1 **orange**
· 1 tablespoon of **balsamic vinegar** (a very
  mild, slightly sweet vinegar, which you
  will find on the oil and vinegar shelf at
  the supermarket)
· 3 tablespoons of **olive oil** (1 for the
  sauce and 2 for cooking with)
· 1 pinch of **salt**

Method

Wash and dry the chives. Using the knife or scissors, cut the stems into the smallest possible sections. Wash the orange thoroughly in cold water and dry it. Cut off three long pieces of peel (zest) using the potato peeler. Cut them into thin strips that are as thin as possible. Cut the orange in half. Squeeze one half and pour the juice into the bowl. If you do not have a lemon squeezer, you can squeeze it by hand. Remove any pits. Add the balsamic vinegar, oil, and salt. Mix them. Get out the plates. Open the kitchen window and shut the door, because salmon gives off a strong smell when cooking. Heat the skillet over a high flame. When it is hot, pour in the oil. To check whether the skillet is hot, pass your hand over it (without actually touching it, of course) or drip a few drops of water onto it: It should smoke and evaporate fairly quickly. When the oil is hot (it takes only about 30 seconds), place the salmon fillets in the pan, with the sides from which the skin was removed (the flat sides) facing down. Cook between 8 and 10 minutes. After two minutes, lower the temperature to a medium heat. The side of the salmon in contact with the pan will become very crunchy, while the other side remains almost raw. To find out if the salmon is cooked sufficiently, touch the upper surface with your finger: If still cold, it needs further cooking. When it becomes nice and warm, you can consider it done. Place the salmon fillets on the plates using the spatula and top them with the strips of orange peel and the chives. Serve with the vinaigrette.

Salmon packages with ginger

Salmon cooked in packages (en papillote) is very creamy and low in fatty oils. Rice (see p. 112), a leek fondue (see p. 120), or potatoes (see p. 116) go very well with this dish.

How long it will take

15 minutes' preparation
+ 10 minutes' cooking time

The equipment you need

- 1 oven
- 1 small bowl
- 1 knife
- 1 tablespoon
- 1 teaspoon
- 3 feet of aluminum foil
- 1 clean dish towel or some paper towels

Optional:

- 1 lemon squeezer

Shopping list

- 2 **salmon fillets** weighing about 5 ounces (150) grams each, with the skin removed. Buy the salmon from a fish store or the fish counter of the supermarket, so you can ask the staff to remove the skin, which is a tricky operation. The highest quality salmon is the wild variety (not farmed); it is more expensive but well worth it.
- 1/2 **lime** (if possible, otherwise an ordinary lemon will do)
- 1 tablespoon of **olive oil**
- 2 teaspoons of powdered **ginger** (you will find it with the other spices and condiments)
- 2 teaspoons of **soy sauce** (a very salty oriental sauce; you will find it on the exotic products shelf in the supermarket, or in an oriental grocery store)
- 10 **cilantro** leaves (a highly aromatic green herb) or 6 stems of chives or 10 leaves of chervil

Method

Remove from the oven the baking tray or broiler pan on which you intend to cook the packages. Set the oven to 425 °F. It takes about 20 minutes for an electric oven

to heat up, 10 minutes for a gas oven (some ovens have an indicator light to tell you when the desired temperature has been reached). Squeeze the 1/2 lime and pour the juice into the bowl. Set aside the equivalent of 1 tablespoon of juice. Add the oil, the ginger, and the soy sauce, and mix well. Prepare the cilantro leaves by plucking them from the stems. Wash and dry them. Tear the aluminum foil so that you have two pieces each 18 inches (50 centimeters) long. Pour roughly a quarter of the sauce onto the middle of the foil and place the salmon on top of it. Pour the same quantity of sauce over the salmon and place 4 cilantro leaves on top. Wrap up the salmon by folding over the edges of the aluminum foil several times, so that the package is hermetically sealed (it is vital to keep all the flavor in). Wrap up the second package in the same way. Place both packages on the baking tray or broiler pan and put them in the oven. Leave them to cook 10 minutes. Then remove the packages from the oven and put them on the plates. Open them up with a knife, and put one fresh cilantro leaf in each package.

Advance preparation

You can prepare the packages earlier in the evening before your guest arrives. Then all you need to do is put them in the oven.

Boneless duck breast with honey and orange sauce

A sweet-and-sour dish that goes well with fresh pasta (see p. 114) or fried mushrooms (see p. 118).

How long it will take

15 minutes' preparation
+ 18 minutes' cooking time

The equipment you need

· 1 small bowl
· 1 saucepan
· 1 tablespoon
· 1 knife
· 1 cooktop with at least 2 burners
· 1 nonstick skillet
· aluminum foil

Shopping list

· 1 **duck breast** (buy ready-packed from the supermarket, or fresh from a poultry dealer)
· 1 **orange** + 1/2 orange for decoration
· 2 tablespoons of **honey**
· 2 tablespoons of **vinegar**
· **salt** and **pepper**
Optional:
· 1 lemon squeezer
· 1 oven
· plastic wrap

Method

Squeeze the orange and pour the juice into the bowl. If you don't have a lemon squeezer, squeeze it by hand. Remove any pits. Add the honey, the vinegar, some salt and pepper, and mix well. Pour this sauce into the saucepan. Lay out the duck, skin side up. Using the knife, make cuts in the skin in a criss-cross pattern. The cuts should be about 1/8 inch (3 millimeters) deep, so that the fat runs out easily during cooking. Open the kitchen window and shut the door, because the duck will smoke during the cooking process. Heat the skillet over a high flame. To check whether the skillet is hot, pass your hand over it or drip a few drops of water onto it; it should smoke and evaporate fairly quickly. When the pan is hot, place the duck in it, skin side down.

Season the duck with salt and pepper on the flesh side. This first stage of the cooking process will take about 10 minutes. After 3 minutes, lower the temperature to a medium flame. At this point, heat the sauce. It should boil slightly, forming small bubbles, and will become thick and syrupy. The duck, meanwhile, will lose a lot of fat. Remove the fat at intervals by pouring it off into the sink. After 10 minutes, lower the flame under the sauce just to keep it warm. Turn over the duck and cook a further 5 minutes. Then leave it to rest 3 minutes on a plate, covered with aluminum foil. This allows the flesh to breathe and become more tender. Cut some slices of orange for decoration. Cut the duck into slices about 1/8 inch (3 millimeters) thick. Place half of these slices on each plate, top with the sauce, and serve.

Advance preparation

You can prepare and cook the sauce the day before. Keep it in the refrigerator in a bowl covered with aluminum foil or plastic wrap. You will just need to reheat it at the last moment. Earlier in the evening, before your guest arrives, you can cook the duck and put it in an ovenproof dish. Cover it with aluminum foil and cook it 7 minutes at 400 °F.

Pork tenderloin, Indonesian style

This dish is reminiscent of the delicious pork brochettes with saté sauce you can order in Indonesian restaurants. The peanut butter gives it an original flavor. The best accompaniment is basmati rice (see p. 112).

How long it will take

15 minutes' preparation
+ 10 minutes' cooking time

The equipment you need

· 1 saucepan
· 1 measuring cup
· 1 tablespoon
· 1 bottle
· 1 sharp knife
· 1 cooktop with at least 2 burners
· 1 nonstick skillet
· 1 fork
Optional:
· 1 lemon squeezer

Shopping list

· 2 **pork tenderloins weighing a total of 8 to 10 ounces** (250 to 300) grams (the meat should be lean and cut fairly thin)
· ½ **lemon**
· ½ cup of **coconut milk** (from the exotic produce shelf of the supermarket, where it is sold in small cardboard cartons or cans, or from an Oriental grocery store)
· 1 tablespoon of **soy sauce** (a very salty oriental sauce; you will find it on the exotic produce shelf in the supermarket, or in an Oriental grocery store)
· 1 handful of **peanuts**
· 2 tablespoons of **oil**
· 1 tablespoon of **peanut butter**
· **salt** and **pepper**

Method

Squeeze the 1/2 lemon over the saucepan. If you don't have a lemon squeezer, do it by hand. Remove any pits. Add the coconut milk, the peanut butter, and the soy sauce, and mix well.

Crush the peanuts by rolling a bottle over them. Cut each piece of pork into 4 lengthwise. Season with salt and pepper. Heat the skillet over a high flame.

When it is hot, pour in the oil. To check whether the skillet is hot, pass your hand over it (without actually touching it, of course) or drip a few drops of water onto it: it should smoke and evaporate fairly quickly. When the oil is hot (it takes only about 30 seconds), place the strips of pork in the pan. After 1 minute, turn them over with the fork and cook a further 1 minute. Then lower the flame to medium heat and cook 4 minutes. Turn the pieces of pork over and continue to cook for another 4 minutes. Meanwhile, heat the sauce over a low flame (it should not be allowed to bubble) about 3 minutes. When the pork is done, place the pieces on the plates, pour the sauce over them, sprinkle with crushed peanuts, and serve.

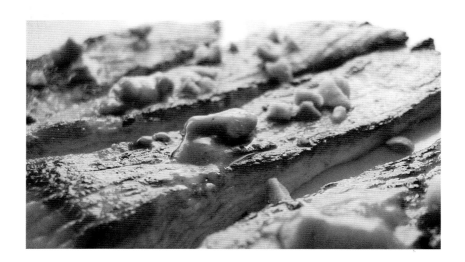

Pork tenderloin with Roquefort

Slow cooking in white wine makes the tenderloin creamy and tender. The Roquefort sauce brings out its flavor and combines well with pasta (see p. 114) or potatoes (see p. 116).

How long it will take

5 minutes' preparation
+ 50 minutes' cooking time

The equipment you need

· 1 measuring cup
· 1 large saucepan
· 1 cooktop
· 1 tablespoon
· 1 fork
· 1 sharp knife
Optional:
· 1 nonstick skillet

Shopping list

· 1 **pork tenderloin** (from the butcher or prepacked from the supermarket)
· roughly 3 ounces (80 grams) **Roquefort** or another blue cheese (calculate the amount in relation to the weight shown on the packaging)
· some **dry white wine** (an inexpensive wine will do for cooking purposes)
· 3 tablespoons of **oil**
· 1/2cup of **light cream**

Method

Pour some white wine into the measuring cup. If the tenderloin is too big to go in the saucepan in one piece, cut it in half. For the following operation, use a nonstick skillet if you have one; otherwise, cook the tenderloin in the saucepan. Heat the skillet or saucepan over a high flame. When it is hot, pour in the oil. To check whether the pan is hot, pass your hand over it (without actually touching it, of course) or drip a few drops of water onto it: it should smoke and evaporate fairly quickly. When the oil is hot (it takes only about 30 seconds), place the tenderloin in the pan.

Brown it all over. This will take about 5 minutes. To turn it over, use a tablespoon and a fork. If you are browning it in the saucepan, it may stick a little, but don't worry. Lower the temperature to a medium heat (if the tenderloin was in the skillet, transfer it to the saucepan), pour in the white wine and leave to cook for 40 minutes. Meanwhile, measure out the cream, break the cheese up with the fork, and get out the plates. When the 40 minutes are up, remove the meat from the saucepan and put it on a plate. Turn up the heat, put the cream and cheese into the saucepan, and continue to cook over a high flame. Cut the meat into slices about 1/3 inch (1 centimeter) thick and put half on each plate. When the sauce is ready, after 3 to 5 minutes (the cheese should be completely melted and the ingredients blended), pour it over the meat. It is ready to serve.

Advance preparation

Earlier in the evening, before your guest arrives, brown the meat.

Fillet of sole meunière

This is a simple but sophisticated dish. The filets will go well with boiled potatoes (see p. 116), rice (see p. 112), or a leek fondue (see p. 120).

How long it will take

10 minutes' preparation
+ 7 minutes' cooking time

The equipment you need

· 1 knife
· 1 small bowl
· 1 tablespoon
· 1 plate
· 1 cooktop
· 1 nonstick skillet
· 1 spatula
· 1 clean dish towel or some paper towels
Optional:
· 1 lemon squeezer
· 1 pair of scissors to cut the herbs

Shopping list

· 4 **sole fillets** (get the fishmonger to fillet the fish, or buy the fillets ready prepared at the supermarket)
· 1 **lemon**
· 5 sprigs of **parsley**
· 4 tablespoons of **flour**
· 2 knobs of **butter**
· **salt** and **pepper**

Method

Wash the lemon thoroughly in cold water and dry it with a dish towel or paper towels. Cut it in half. Squeeze 1 half and pour the juice into the bowl. If you don't have a lemon squeezer, you can squeeze it by hand. Remove any pits.
Set aside the equivalent of 2 tablespoons of juice. Cut the other half of the lemon

into thin slices. Wash and dry the parsley, then cut it into small pieces. Pour the flour onto a plate. Place the sole fillets in the flour, so they are covered with a thin white coating. Season them on both sides with salt and pepper. Get out the plates. Heat the skillet over a high flame. When it is hot, put 1 knob of butter in the pan. To check whether the skillet is hot, pass your hand over it (without actually touching it, of course) or drip a few drops of water onto it; it should smoke and evaporate fairly quickly. When the butter has melted and begins to sputter, place the sole fillets in the pan.

Cook 2 to 3 minutes, then turn them over with a spatula and cook a further 2 to 3 minutes. They should be a nice golden color. Place the sole fillets on the plates. Put the second knob of butter in the hot pan. Pour the lemon juice on the fillets. As soon as the butter has melted, pour it on the sole fillets. Spread the herbs and lemon slices over the fish and serve.

Pasta with lemon and Parmesan

The lemon gives this pasta dish an unusual zingy taste.

How long it will take

15 minutes' preparation + the cooking time shown on the pack containing the pasta

The equipment you need

- 1 potato peeler
- 1 bowl for serving the Parmesan
- 1 clean dish towel or some paper towels
- 1 knife
- 1 small bowl for the lemon juice
- 2 saucepans, 1 big and 1 small
- 1 measuring cup
- 1 cooktop with at least 2 burners
- 1 fork
- 1 colander (otherwise, use a plate or lid slightly bigger than the saucepan when pouring away the hot water; hold the plate or lid with a dish towel and take care not to scald your hands)
- 1 tablespoon

Optional:
- 1 lemon squeezer

Shopping list

- about 5 ounces (160 grams) of dry **pasta**: fusilli, penne, or spaghetti (i.e. roughly one third of a 16 ounce (500 gram) pack)
- about 2 ½ ounces (75 grams) of **Parmesan** (i.e. ½ cup of Parmesan grated with the potato peeler, or ⅓ cup of ready-grated parmesan)
- 1 **lemon**
- ½ cupr of **light cream**
- 1 teaspoon of **salt** for the water in which you cook the pasta

Method

If you have bought a piece of parmesan, grate it with the potato peeler to obtain slivers of cheese. Put the Parmesan in a bowl to serve at the table.
Wash the lemon thoroughly and dry it with a dish towel or some paper towels. Peel

off 3 long strips of zest (peel) with the potato peeler. Cut them into thinner strips about 1/8 inch (1 millimeter) thick. Cut the lemon in half. Squeeze it and pour the juice into the bowl. Remove any pits. Put a large saucepan of water on the cooktop to boil, with the teaspoon of salt. When it is boiling hard, add the pasta. Let it cook for the time shown on the packaging. Five minutes before it is ready, pour the light cream into the small saucepan with the strips of lemon and heat over a medium flame. When the pasta is ready (spear a piece with a fork and bite it to check), drain off the water, and put the pasta back in the saucepan. Pour 2 tablespoons of lemon juice over it and turn. Then pour on the hot cream with the strips of lemon and turn again. Put half of the pasta on each plate and serve. Bring the grated Parmesan to the table so that your guests can help herself.

Lamb chops with a yogurt and mint sauce

Crunchy, well-browned lamb chops with a cool aromatic sauce. You can serve this dish with potatoes (see p. 116), slow-fried zucchini (p. 122), or green beans (p. 124).

How long it will take

15 minutes' preparation
+ 6 minutes' cooking time

The equipment you need

· 1 knife
· 1 bowl
· 1 clean dish towel or some paper towels
· 1 cooktop
· 1 nonstick skillet
· 1 teaspoon

Shopping list

· 4 **lamb chops**
· 1 small **yogurt** (slightly liquid, the Greek type); for a lighter version of this recipe, buy a yogurt containing 0 % fat
· 1 **clove of garlic** (if you prefer not to peel and cut garlic, use 1 teaspoon of frozen garlic or garlic powder)
· 12 **mint leaves** or 12 **basil leaves** or 12 **cilantro leaves** or 20 stems of chives
· 2 tablespoons of **olive oil**
· **salt** and **pepper**

Method

Prepare the clove of garlic by cutting and removing the outer dry layer of skin. Cut it in half lengthwise. Place each half flat side down and cut it into thin slices. Then chop the slices into small pieces. Wash and dry the mint leaves. Set 2 aside for decorative purposes and cut the others into thin strips. Pour the yogurt into a bowl, add the garlic and the mint, and mix. Add salt and pepper a little at a time, tasting now and again to make sure you are not overdoing it.

Season the lamb chops on both sides with salt and pepper. Open the kitchen window and shut the door, because the meat will smoke while cooking. Heat the skillet over a high flame. When it is hot, pour in the oil. To check whether the skillet is hot, pass your hand over it (without actually touching it, of course) or drip a few drops of water onto it; it should smoke and evaporate fairly quickly. When the oil is hot (it takes only about 30 seconds), place the lamb chops in the pan. Fry them about 3 minutes on either side. They should be well browned and crisp on the outside, pink in the middle (unless you prefer them well done, in which case increase the cooking time to 5 minutes per side). Place 2 chops on each plate, pour some of the yogurt sauce alongside them, and decorate with the whole mint leaves. The dish is ready to serve.

Tuna carpaccio

A variation on the carpaccio (thinly sliced raw meat or fish) theme, using tuna rather than beef. Half-size portions can also be served as an appetizer.

How long it will take

30 minutes

The equipment you need

- 1 potato peeler
- 1 sharp knife
- 1 clean dish towel or some paper towels
- 1 tablespoon
- 1 measuring cup
- 1 small bowl

Optional:

- 1 pair of scissors for cutting up the chives
- plastic wrap

Shopping list

- 12 ounces (340 grams) of **tuna fillet, skinned and without bones. Buy the tuna from a fish store or from the fish counter in the supermarket. Ask the staff to remove the skin, because this is a tricky operation.**
- 1/2 cup of **Parmesan cheese, grated with a potato peeler (approx. 75 grams)**
- 10 stems of **chives**
- 3 tablespoons of **olive oil**
- 1 tablespoon of **balsamic vinegar** (a very mild, slightly sweet vinegar you will find on the oil and vinegar shelf in the supermarket)

Method

If there is a freezer compartment in your refrigerator, put the fish in it for 30 minutes: It will be easier to slice. Slice the Parmesan with the potato peeler to obtain slivers of the cheese. Cut the fish into the thinnest possible slices. Put half on each plate. Wash and dry the stems of chives, and cut them into pieces about 1/8 inch (3 millimeters) long, using the knife or scissors.

Mix the oil and vinegar in the bowl, and pour the mixture over the tuna slices. Sprinkle the chives and parmesan over the top. The carpaccio is ready to serve.

Advance preparation
Earlier in the evening, before your guest arrives, prepare the carpaccio and keep it in the refrigerator, having covered the plates with plastic wrap.

Chicken salad with blue cheese

A popular salad, substantial enough to present as a main dish.

How long it will take

15 minutes' preparation
+ 20 minutes' cooking time

The equipment you need

- 1 knife
- 1 small bowl
- 1 saucepan or 1 nonstick skillet
- 1 cooktop
- 1 tablespoon
- paper towels
- 1 salad bowl
Optional:
- 1 lemon squeezer
- plastic wrap
- 1 clean dish towel

Shopping list

- 2 **chicken breasts** (the white meat), skinless
- 1 handful of **grapes/raisins** (depending on the season)
- ½ **lemon**
- 5 tablespoons of **oil**
- 2 tablespoons of **vinegar**
- 1 tablespoon of **French's mustard** (a yellow, fairly mild and sweet kind of mustard) or 1 teaspoon of Dijon mustard
- about 4 ounces (110 grams) of **blue cheese**; calculate the amount in relation to the weight shown on the packaging)
- 3 handfuls of **lettuce** (you can buy it ready-washed in a bag)
- **salt** and **pepper**

Method

Cut the lemon in half. Squeeze ½ and pour the juice into the bowl. If you don't have a lemon squeezer, you can do it by hand. Remove any pits. Put the saucepan or skillet on the stove to heat over a very low flame. Pour in 1 tablespoon of oil. When the oil is well warmed, place the chicken breasts in the pan and pour the lemon juice over them.

Season with salt and pepper. Let them cook 10 minutes on either side. The flesh should become white, but not brown (if it does begin to brown, turn down the heat). Meanwhile, mix the vinegar in the bowl with the mustard and the remainder of the oil. Cut the cheese into small dice about 1/3 inch (1 centimeter) square.

When the chicken is done, leave it to cool down, then cut it into dice, also about ⅓ inch (1 centimeter) square. If you bought the lettuce in a bag, it is already washed. If not, wash it in cold water and dry it with a dish towel or paper towels. Put the lettuce in the salad bowl and mix it with the sauce. Now divide the seasoned salad between the two plates, and top it with the grapes/raisins, cheese dice, and chicken dice.

Advance preparation

The chicken breasts can be cooked the day before. Keep them whole in the refrigerator, in some plastic wrap, so that they do not dry out.

Penne with Gorgonzola and walnuts

A quick but flavorsome pasta recipe. The crunchiness of the nuts enhances the appeal.

How long it will take

10 minutes' preparation + the cooking time indicated on the pack containing the pasta

The equipment you need

- 1 knife
- 2 saucepans: 1 large and 1 small
- 1 cooktop with at least 2 burners
- 1 measuring cup
- 1 tablespoon
- 1 colander (otherwise, use a plate or lid slightly bigger than the saucepan when straining off the hot water: hold the plate or lid with a dish towel and take care not to scald your hands)
- 1 fork for testing the pasta to see if it is cooked

Shopping list

- about 5 ounces (160) grams of **penne or another tubular form of pasta (roughly ⅓ of a 16 ounce** 500 gram pack). The advantage of penne is that they are short, and easy to eat without making a mess
- 8 **walnut** kernels (the edible part of the nut which remains when you remove the shell; you will find them on the home-baking shelf in the supermarket, or with the dried or fresh fruit)
- About 3 ½ ounces (100) grams of **Gorgonzola** (an Italian blue cheese) or similar; calculate the amount in relation to the weight shown on the packaging
- ½ cup of **light cream**
- 1 teaspoon of **salt** to go in the water for cooking the pasta

Method

Break the walnut kernels into quarters with your fingers. Cut about a quarter of the Gorgonzola into small dice and set them aside. Put a large saucepan of water on to boil, having added the salt. When the water is boiling hard, add the penne. Leave them to cook for the time indicated on the packaging. Five minutes before they are done, pour the light cream into the small saucepan with the remainder of the Gorgonzola and heat over a medium flame. Stir with a spoon to make sure that the sauce is evenly blended. When the penne is cooked (try a bit to check), strain the water off, and return them to the saucepan. Pour the light cream and Gorgonzola mixture over them and stir. Top the pasta with the pieces of walnut and the gorgonzola dice.

Corn salad, apple, and smoked duck-breast salad

This salad is substantial enough to form a main dish.

How long it will take

15 minutes' preparation
+ 5 minutes' cooking time

The equipment you need

- 1 dish towel or some paper towels
- 1 salad bowl or 1 large bowl
- 1 small bowl
- 1 tablespoon
- 1 teaspoon
- 1 knife
- 1 potato peeler
- 1 cooktop
- 1 nonstick skillet
- 1 spatula or 1 fork

Shopping list

- 3 handfuls of **corn salad** (also known as **lamb's lettuce** or **mache**), ready washed in a bag (or other green salad leaves)
- 10 **walnut kernels** (the edible part of the nut which remains when you remove the shell; you will find them on the home-baking shelf in the supermarket, or with the dried or fresh fruit)
- about 3 ½ ounces (100 grams) of **smoked or dried duck breast** in slices (it is sold vacuum packed in supermarkets), or 3 ½ ounces (100 grams) of **bacon lardoons**, or **pancetta**
- 1 teaspoon of **Dijon mustard**
- 1 tablespoon of **vinegar**
- 3 tablespoons of oil
- ½ **apple**
- 1 pinch of **salt**
- 1 pinch of **pepper**

Method

If you bought the corn salad in a bag, it will be ready washed. If not, wash it in cold water and dry with a dish towel or some paper towels. Remove the small white roots with your fingers; it looks better that way. Put the corn salad in a salad bowl. Break the walnut kernels into halves and place them on the salad leaves. Remove the slices of duck breast (or the lardoons or pancetta) from their packaging. In the small bowl, mix the Dijon mustard, vinegar, and salt, using a spoon.

Add 1 tablespoon of oil and mix again. The mixture should be well blended.

Repeat this process with the 2 remaining spoonfuls of oil. Then add in the pinch of pepper and mix again. When the time comes to serve the dish, cut the 1/2 apple into 4 segments. Peel them with the potato peeler and remove the core. Then cut each slice into 5 or 6 small pieces. Place them on the salad, pour the vinaigrette over it, and mix. Get the pla-

tes out and put half of the salad on each. Heat the skillet over a high flame. To check whether it is hot, pass your hand over it (without actually touching it, of course) or drip a few drops of water onto it; it should smoke and evaporate fairly quickly. Place the slices of duck breast (or the lardoons or pancetta) in the pan and fry them, turning them over once with the spatula or the fork until the fat is a nice golden color. This should take 3 to 4 minutes (slightly longer for the lardoons or pancetta). Put half on each plate, with the salad. The meal is ready to serve.

Chicken in a Parmesan crust

The breaded chicken is crisp and golden, its taste set off by the Parmesan. This dish can be served with a green salad, slow-fried zucchini (see p. 122), or green beans (see p. 124).

How long it will take

25 minutes' preparation
+ 6 minutes' cooking time

The equipment you need

- 1 small bowl
- 2 plates
- 1 fork
- 1 knife
- 1 measuring cup
- 1 tablespoon
- 1 saucepan
- 1 nonstick skillet
- 1 spatula
- 1 cooktop

Shopping list

- 2 **chicken breasts** (the white meat)
- ½ to 1 cup of **grated Parmesan** (roughly 100 to 200 grams; you can find it in the prepacked cheese section of the supermarket)
- ½ to 1 cup of **breadcrumbs** (sold ready prepared) or 4 rusks
- 1 **egg**
- ½ **lemon**
- ½ cup of **ketchup**
- 1 tablespoon of **honey**
- 3 tablespoons of **balsamic vinegar** (a very mild vinegar you will find on the oil and vinegar shelf in the supermarket)
- 2 tablespoons of **olive oil**
- **salt** and **pepper**

Method

Pour the breadcrumbs into the bowl. Add the grated Parmesan and mix thoroughly. Spread the resulting mixture on a plate. Break the egg into the bowl and beat it with a fork to blend the white and the yolk. Using your fingers, remove the skin (if there is any) from the chicken breasts.

Cut them in 4 pieces lengthwise. Season with salt and pepper. Cut the ½ lemon into 2 pieces. Using your fingers, dip the slices of chicken into the beaten egg, making sure each slice is well soaked, then dip them in the breadcrumbs so that each piece is well coated. Place them on a plate. Pour the ketchup, the honey, and the balsamic vinegar into a saucepan, mix the ingredients, and heat them gently. Heat the skillet over a medium flame. When it is hot, pour in the oil. To check whether it is hot, pass your hand over it (without actually touching it, of course) or drip a few drops of water onto it; it should smoke and evaporate fairly quickly. When the oil is hot (it takes only about 30 seconds), place the slices of chicken in the pan. Fry them about 3 minutes on either side, until they are a nice golden color. Turn them over carefully using the spatula and the tablespoon. Place 4 slices of chicken on each plate with a lemon quarter, pour the hot sauce alongside them, and serve immediately.

Accompaniments

Personal experiences

Annie called me
the prince of vinaigrette,
the salad king, no less…
**Larry, 55, chief
executive**

Good old
pasta again… Yes,
but this time it did not
all stick together. Much
classier.
**Frank, 32, dog
breeder**

Emma
blushed and said:
"And I took you for
a guy with no practical
ability."
**Patrick (19),
student**

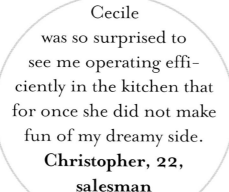

Cecile was so surprised to see me operating effi-ciently in the kitchen that for once she did not make fun of my dreamy side.

Christopher, 22, salesman

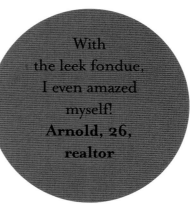

With the leek fondue, I even amazed myself!

Arnold, 26, realtor

Salad

You can buy mixed leaves ready prepared in a bag. This is very convenient because they do not need washing. More and more varieties are available: young leaves, salad mixtures, lettuce hearts, arugula... Reckon on between 2 and 3 1/2 ounces (60 and 100) grams for 2 people, or 2 large handfuls. If you buy a whole lettuce, you will have to prepare it. First, cut off the leaves with a knife and throw away any that are spoiled or damaged. Then wash the leaves you have kept in cold water, taking care to remove any dirt. Dry the leaves with a clean dish towel or with paper towels. If you have a salad spinner (you never know!), you can of course use it to give them a spin. Tear the leaves by hand into pieces that will not need to be cut again before they are eaten. If your prepare your salad the day before, keep it in a plastic bag in the refrigerator.

Vinaigrette dressing

Ingredients

· 1 teaspoon of strong **Dijon mustard**
· 1 tablespoon of **red wine vinegar**
· 3 tablespoons of **oil** (sunflower or groundnut type)
· 1 pinch of **salt**
· 1 pinch of **pepper**

A basic recipe

In a small bowl, or directly in the salad bowl, mix the mustard, the vinegar, and the salt using a spoon. Add 1 tablespoon of oil, and mix again. The mixture should be fairly well blended. Repeat the process with the 2 remaining spoonfuls of oil. Then mix in the pinch of pepper (if you put the pepper in earlier, it will lose its taste because of the vinegar).

For a bit of a change
Use olive oil, walnut oil, etc. These oils have a stronger taste. Try them first to see if you like them. You can also try using balsamic vinegar (a very mild, slightly sweet vinegar you will find on the oil and vinegar shelf in the supermarket) or sherry vinegar, cider vinegar, raspberry vinegar, etc. The Dijon mustard can be replaced with a whole-grain mustard, or a herbal version, tarragon mustard for example.

Simplified version
This vinaigrette can be made at the last moment, just before you serve the salad. All you need is oil and vinegar. Put the leaves in the salad bowl. Pour 3 tablespoons of oil over them. Mix well, so that the leaves are well coated with oil, then pour on 1 tablespoon of vinegar, and mix again. For an Italian-style dressing, use olive oil and balsamic vinegar.

A very light salad dressing
Replace the oil with some 0 % fat yogurt, and the vinegar with lemon juice.

Just before serving
If you prepare the vinaigrette in advance, the oil and vinegar will undoubtedly separate. This is quite normal; all you need to do is stir it again. Mix the salad leaves with the dressing at the very last moment, otherwise the leaves will go limp. Do not overfill the salad bowl, or the salad will spill over the sides.

Rice

The equipment you need

- 1 saucepan
- 1 cooktop
- 1 serving dish
- 1 colander (otherwise, use a plate or lid slightly bigger than the saucepan when straining off the hot water; hold them with a dish towel and take care not to scald your hands)
- 1 fork for tasting the rice while it is cooking

Shopping list

- **rice**: about 1/4 cup (50 grams) for 2 people as an accompaniment. You can buy quick-cooking rice, which is easy and convenient to use. For something more sophisticated, choose basmati rice, which is more aromatic and has attractive-looking long grains.
- 1 tablespoon of **salt** to add to the cooking water

Optional:
- 1 small knob of **butter**

Method

When cooking rice, the best advice is to follow the instructions printed on the packaging: Every sort of rice has a different cooking time. Taste the rice when the stated time is nearly up; if it is not done enough, cook it a bit longer. After draining it and putting it in the serving dish, you can add a small knob of butter to make it smoother (but it will also be richer).

Advance preparation

Earlier in the evening, before your guest arrives, cook the rice and drain it, but do not add the knob of butter. A few minutes before serving, pour 1 tablespoon of water into the saucepan with the rice and reheat over a low flame, adding the knob of butter and stirring, to prevent the rice from sticking. The best way to check whether it is hot enough is to test it with your finger.

Pasta

The equipment you need

· 1 large saucepan
· 1 fork for tasting the pasta to see if it is cooked
· 1 cooktop
· 1 colander (otherwise, use a plate or lid slightly bigger than the saucepan when straining off the hot water; hold the plate or lid with a dish towel and take care not to scald your hands)

Shopping list

· **dry pasta**: about 4 ounces (120 grams) for 2 people as an accompaniment (i.e. 1/4 of a 16 ounce pack), or 5 ounces (150 grams) for 2 people as a main dish (i.e. roughly 1/3 of a pack)
· **fresh pasta**: about 1/2 pound (200 grams) for 2 people as an accompaniment, or 10 ounces (300 grams) for 2 people as a main dish
· 1 tablespoon of **salt** to add to the water you cook it in

Method

When cooking pasta, the best thing is to follow the instructions printed on the packaging. It is important to cook pasta in plenty of water; use a larger saucepan. Wait until the water is boiling hard before you put in the pasta. Fresh pasta is convenient, because it cooks very quickly (2 to 4 minutes). It is normally displayed in the fresh produce section at the supermarket. Taste the pasta when the stated cooking time is nearly up: If it is still too hard, let it cook for a bit longer. It is not a good idea to prepare pasta in advance because it tends to stick.

Boiled potatoes

One of the easiest ways to cook potatoes.

How long it will take

20 to 30 minutes' cooking time

The equipment you need

- 1 saucepan
- 1 cooktop
- 1 knife for pricking the potatoes to see if they are done
- 1 colander for straining the water from the potatoes or 1 tablespoon for lifting them out of the saucepan

Shopping list

- **potatoes:** about 1 pound (500) grams for 2 people. Choose a smaller variety or new potatoes: They are delicious and, since they have very thin skins, there is no need to peel them
- 1 tablespoon of **salt** to add to the water you cook them in

Optional:
- some **butter** on the table

Method

Wash the potatoes in cold water, put them in the saucepan and fill it with water so that the potatoes are well covered. Add the salt. Heat the saucepan over a high flame until the water begins to boil. Start timing at this point. After 15 minutes (10 minutes if using very small potatoes), prick a potato with the knife. If it penetrates easily, the potatoes are cooked. If not, repeat the operation 5 minutes later, and so on until they are of the right consistency. This should not take more than 20 minutes, but the time will depend on the size of the potatoes. When the potatoes are done, strain them using the colander, or lift them from the saucepan with a spoon, and serve them piping hot.

Put some butter on the table because potatoes are delicious with butter melted

over them. But this is not essential if the dish they are accompanying has its own sauce.

Advance preparation

Earlier in the evening, before your guest arrives, you can cook and drain the potatoes. When the time comes to serve them, reheat them gently in the saucepan with 1 tablespoon of water to stop them from drying out.

Panfried mushrooms

Mushrooms done in this way can be served with meat, poultry, or fish. The two-stage cooking process is quick and insures that all the flavor is retained.

How long it will take

5 minutes' preparation
+ 10 minutes' cooking time

The equipment you need

· 1 clean dish towel or some paper towels
· 1 small knife
· 1 colander
· 1 cooktop
· 1 nonstick skillet
· 1 spatula or 1 wooden spoon
Optional:
· 1 pair of scissors

Shopping list

· ½ pound (200 grams) of **button mushrooms** (the easiest to find all the year round);
· 10 stems of **chives** (or 10 stems of parsley)
· 1 tablespoon of **oil**
· 1 knob of **butter** (a piece the size of a walnut)
· ½ teaspoon of **salt**

Method

Wash and dry the herbs. Set aside 2 or 3 whole pieces for decoration. Cut up the others with the knife or a pair of scissors. Quickly rinse the mushrooms in cold water to remove any dirt, but do not let them soak up any water. Cut the end off the stalk of each mushroom, then cut them into slices about 1/8 inch (3 millimeters) thick, vertically, from the cap to the base. Position the colander in the sink. Heat the skillet over a medium flame. When it is hot, pour in the oil.

To check whether the skillet is hot, pass your hand over it (without actually touching it, of course) or drip a few drops of water onto it; it should smoke and evaporate fairly quickly. When the oil is hot (it takes only about 30 seconds), put the mushrooms in the pan. Season with salt and cook about 3 minutes, turning them with the spatula or a wooden spoon, until they begin to release water. Pour them into the colander and allow them to drain 5 minutes. Now put the

skillet back on the cooktop (no need to wash it first), melt the knob of butter over a medium flame, then add in the mushrooms. Leave them to cook 5 minutes. Sprinkle with the herbs. The mushrooms are ready to serve.

Advance preparation
Before your guest arrives, cut up the herbs and cook the mushrooms in the oil. Drain them. When the time comes to serve them, all you need do is cook them in the butter.

Leek fondue

Leek fondue goes particularly well with fish dishes, but can also be served with white meats and poultry.

How long it will take

5 minutes' preparation

+ 25 minutes' cooking time

Advance preparation

· You can prepare the leek fondue earlier in the evening, before your guest arrives. When the time comes to serve it, all you need do is reheat it gently.

The equipment you need

· 1 knife
· 1 cooktop
· 1 skillet or 1 saucepan

Shopping list

· 4 **leeks**
· 1 knob of **butter** (a piece the size of a walnut)
· **salt** and **pepper**

Method

Cut off the dark green sections of the leeks and discard. Slice off the end of the root. Split the leeks in half lengthwise. Remove the outer layer, then wash them in cold water to remove any dirt. Cut them into sections roughly 1/3 inch (1 centimeter) long. Melt the knob of butter in the skillet or in a saucepan over a low flame, then add the leeks. Season with salt and pepper. Let them cook 15 minutes, stirring from time to time. They will become soft and transparent.

Advance preparation

You can prepare the leek fondue earlier in the evening, before your guest arrives. When the time comes to serve it, all you need do is reheat it gently.

Slow-fried zucchini

Zucchini cooked slowly and gently in this way are very smooth and tasty. They are an excellent accompaniment for fish dishes.

How long it will take

10 minutes' preparation
+ roughly 1 hour's cooking time

The equipment you need

- 1 clean dish towel or some paper towels
- 1 knife
- 1 cooktop
- 1 nonstick skillet
- 1 spatula
- 1 tablespoon

Optional:
- some aluminum foil or plastic wrap
- 1 bowl

Shopping list

- 2 **zucchini**
- 3 tablespoons of **olive oil**
- 1 tablespoon de **balsamic vinegar** (a very mild vinegar you will find on the oil and vinegar shelf in the supermarket)
- **salt** and **pepper**

Method

Rinse the zucchini in cold water and dry them with a dish towel or some paper towels. Cut off and throw away both ends, then cut the remainder into slices about 1/4 inch (5 millimeters) thick. Heat the skillet over a low flame. Pour in the oil, then add the sliced zucchini. Season with salt and pepper. Leave them to cook about 1 hour, turning them occasionally with the spatula to insure that all the slices are cooked equally. They will become very soft, and some may even break up. This is quite normal.

Two minutes before you finish cooking the zucchini, add the balsamic vinegar and

stir it in. Before serving, taste to check that it is sufficiently seasoned, and add more salt or pepper if necessary.

Advance preparation
You can cook the zucchini the day before, but without adding the balsamic vinegar. Keep them in the refrigerator, in a bowl covered with aluminum foil or plastic wrap. In the evening, reheat them gently with the vinegar.

Crunchy green beans

Young green beans coated in crunchy breadcrumbs: a real delight!

How long it will take

20 minutes' preparation
+ 17 minutes' cooking time

The equipment you need

· I clean dish towel or some paper
  towels
· I cooktop
· I large saucepan
· I colander (otherwise, use a plate or
  lid slightly bigger than the saucepan
  when straining off the hot water; hold
  the plate or lid with a dish towel and
  take care not to scald your hands)
· I skillet
· I tablespoon
· I teaspoon

Shopping list

· I/2 pound (200 grams) of very young,
  small **green beans** (2 large handfuls);
  these have no stringy bits and are easier
  to prepare
· 3 tablespoons of **breadcrumbs** (buy
  them ready to use)
· I knob of **butter** (a piece the size of
  a walnut)
· I teaspoon of **salt**

Method

Wash and dry the beans. Using your fingers, break off either end of each bean (or cut off with a knife if easier). Put a large saucepan of water on the stove to boil. When it is boiling hard, add the beans. Leave them to cook 12 minutes, then drain them. Heat the skillet over a medium flame. To check whether it is hot, pass your hand over it (without actually touching it, of course) or drip a few drops of water onto it; it should smoke and evaporate fairly quickly. When the pan is hot, pour

in the breadcrumbs, add the butter. and stir with the tablespoon.
When the breadcrumbs are a nice golden color (roughly 2 minutes), add the beans and the salt, and cook a further 3 minutes, coating the beans with the breadcrumbs.

Advance preparation
Earlier in the evening, before your guest arrives, you can boil the beans and drain them. When the time comes to serve them, follow the recipe from this stage. It may be necessary to reheat the beans in the bread-crumbs for a rather longer period to insure that they are nice and hot.

Desserts

Personal experiences

The pastries with hazelnut spread and banana melted Sophie's heart.
Patrick, 25, police officer

And suddenly, there I was: the Casanova of the kitchen!
Alan, 42, farm manager

While she was trying the apple tartlet I finally plucked up the courage to ask her to marry me. She said yes!
Philip, 28, product manager

A salad bowl, a tablespoon, a knife… and a wide-eyed guest.
George, 34, cameraman

Frankly, I had already scored points with the appetizer and the main dish, but with the apple crunchies I think it was game, set, and match.
Tony, 33, high school teacher

Apple crunchies with raisins and honey

In this recipe, the crunchiness of the phyllo pastry contrasts nicely with the creamy smoothness of the cooked apple.

How long it will take

10 minutes' preparation + about 10 minutes' cooking time for the apples + 6 minutes' cooking time for the phyllo pastry

The equipment you need

- 1 knife
- 1 potato peeler
- 1 cooktop
- 1 nonstick skillet
- 1 tablespoon
- 1 clean dish towel or some paper towels
- 1 spatula
- 3 plates

Shopping list

- 1 **apple**
- 2 knobs of **butter** (each the size of a walnut)
- 1 handful of **raisins**
- 1 tablespoon of **honey**
- 2 **squares of phyllo dough** (very thin sheets of dough, which you will find on the same shelf as the ready-to-bake dough in the supermarket, or in oriental grocers; they come in packs of 10, but can be kept for quite a long time)

Optional:

- 2 tablespoons of **light cream** (not ideal for dieters, but very nice!)
- 2 **mint** leaves of for decoration

Method

Cut the apple into 8 segments. Peel them with the potato peeler and remove the core from each segment. Cut each segment into 5 or 6 smaller pieces. Melt 1 knob of butter in the skillet, over a low flame, and add the pieces of apple and the raisins. Let them cook 10 minutes, then add the honey.

Mix it in and continue to cook 1 minute. Remove the apple from the pan with a spoon and leave it to cool on a plate. Wash and dry the pan with a dish towel or some paper towels. Get out the squares of phyllo dough. They are separated by sheets of paper to prevent them from sticking together. Take one of them, very carefully because they are fragile, and place it on the second plate. Place half of the cooked apple in the middle of the dough sheet and fold in the edges of the dough to form a square envelope. Repeat the operation with a second dough sheet, using another plate. Melt the remaining knob of butter in the skillet, over a medium flame, and gently place the two "envelopes" in it, folded side down. Leave them to cook 3 minutes. The dough will become crunchy and golden in color. Gently turn the "envelopes" over with the spatula and cook a further 2 minutes. If the butter is too hot and the pastries begin to burn, turn down the heat. Cut each envelope in half to form 2 triangles. You can, if you like, now add 1 spoonful of light cream per person and decorate with a mint leaf. To eat this dessert, you may need a knife and fork.

Advance preparation
You can prepare the "envelopes" before your guest arrives.

Caramelized clementines with vanilla ice cream

The hot, slightly acidic clementines make a surprising contrast with the ice cream.

How long it will take

5 minutes' preparation
+ 10 minutes' cooking time

The equipment you need

- 1 freezer compartment for keeping the ice cream
- 1 cooktop
- 1 nonstick skillet
- 1 spatula
- 1 tablespoon

Shopping list

- 4 balls of **vanilla ice cream**
- 3 **clementines** (preferably seedless)
- 1 knob of butter (a piece the size of a walnut)
- 1 tablespoon of **sugar**

Method

Take the ice cream out of the freezer to let it soften a little. Peel the clementines and break them up into segments. Melt the butter in the skillet over a low flame. When it is melted, add the clementine segments. Cook 3 minutes then turn them over gently with the spatula. Continue to cook a further 3 minutes. Sprinkle the segments with sugar and cook a further 2 minutes on either side. Remove the skillet from the cooktop. Put the vanilla ice cream in bowls or plates. Place the clementine segments around the ice cream and serve immediately.

Puff pastries with banana and hazelnut spread

A dessert to make your mouth water; it will become a firm favorite

How long it will take

10 minutes' preparation + 10 minutes' baking time (in the oven) + 5 minutes' cooking time in the skillet

The equipment you need

· 1 refrigerator with feezing compartment
· 1 bottle
· 1 small bowl
· 1 knife
· 1 oven
· 1 baking tray or ovenproof broiler pan
· baking parchment roll or sheet
· 1 cooktop
· 1 nonstick skillet
· 1 spatula
· 1 tablespoon
Optional:
· 1 teaspoon

Shopping list

· 1 package of ready-to-bake frozen **puff pastry**
· 2 tablespoons of **hazelnut spread**
· 1 **banana**
· 1 knob of **butter** (a piece the size of a walnut)
Optional:
· 2 teaspoons of **flaked coconut** (you will find it on the baking ingredients shelf in the supermarket)

Method

Defrost the package of puff pastry in the microwave to allow it to soften and make it easier to unroll (or remove from the refrigerator if you have placed it there the day before). Also have the hazelnut spread to hand. Remove from the oven the baking tray or broiler pan on which you intend to cook the pastries and line it with parchment paper. Heat the oven to 400 °F. It takes 20 minutes for an electric oven to heat up, 10 minutes for a gas oven (some ovens have a light which goes off when the desired temperature has been reached). Roll out the dough using the bottle. Place the small bowl rim down on the dough, very near the edge, and press hard to cut out a circular piece. If it does not come away cleanly, cut it out with a knife. Repeat this step for the second pastry and remove the excess dough.

When the oven has reached the right temperature, place the pastries on the baking tray or broiler pan, and put them in the oven. Leave them to cook 10 minutes. In the meanwhile, peel the banana and cut it into sections about 1/4 inch (5 millimeters) in length. If the pastry begins to burn, turn down the oven to 350 °F. When they are done, remove the pastries from the oven and slide them onto the plates. Allow them to cool down. Meanwhile, melt the butter in the skillet, over a

low flame. When it is melted, add the slices of banana. Cook them 3 minutes, then turn them over with the spatula and cook a further 2 minutes. Spread 1 tablespoon of hazelnut spread over each pastry, then place the banana sections on top. To add a slightly exotic touch, you can sprinkle each biscuit with 1 teaspoon of flaked coconut.

Advance preparation
The puff paste pastries can be cooked the day before. Keep them in a dry environment.

Apple tartlets

You do not need a pie dish to produce this delicious small-scale version of apple pie.

How long it will take

15 minutes' preparation + 25 minutes' cooking time

The equipment you need

- 1 oven
- 1 baking tray or 1 ovenproof broiler pan
- baking parchment roll or sheet
- 1 bottle
- 1 sharp knife
- 1 potato peeler
- 1 small bowl
- 1 tablespoon
- 1 teaspoon

Shopping list

- 1 package of ready-to-bake frozen **puff pastry**
- 1 large **apple** or 2 small apples
- 1 knob of **butter** (a piece the size of a walnut)
- 2 tablespoons of **sugar**
Optional:
- 1 teaspoon of **cinnamon**

Method

Defrost the package of puff pastry in the microwave to allow it to soften and make it easier to roll out (or remove from the refrigerator if you have placed it there the day before). Remove from the oven the baking tray or broiler pan in which you intend to cook the tartlets and line with parchment paper. Heat the oven to 400 °F. It takes 20 minutes for an electric oven to heat up, 10 minutes for a gas oven (some ovens have a light which goes off when the desired temperature has been reached). Cut the apple into quarters. Peel them with the potato peeler and remove the core from each quarter using the knife. Then cut them into the thinnest possible slices. Roll out the dough using the bottle. Place the small bowl rim down on the dough, very near the edge, and press hard to cut out a circular piece. If it does not come away cleanly, cut it out with the knife. Repeat this step for the second tartlet.

Remove the excess dough. Place the slices of apple on each tartlet, in overlapping circles (like a rosette). Cut the knob of butter into thin slivers and spread them over each tartlet, and sprinkle each tartlet with 1 tablespoon of sugar. When the oven has reached the right temperature, place the tartlets on the baking tray or broiler pan and put them in the oven. Bake for 25 minutes. Check how they are doing after 20 minutes. If the pastry begins to burn, lower the oven temperature to 350 °F . When they are done, remove the tartlets from the oven and slide them onto the plates. If you like, you can sprinkle them with cinnamon. The dessert is ready.

Advance preparation

If you don't have a microwave, place the puff pastry dough in the refrigerator the day before to defrost. You can prepare the tartlets earlier in the evening, before your guest arrives, and put them in the oven during the meal.

Orange fruit salad

A refreshing dessert, aromatic and very light.

How long it will take

15 minutes' preparation

The equipment you need

- 1 clean dish towel or some paper towels
- 1 potato peeler
- 1 sharp knife
- 1 tablespoon
- 1 teaspoon

Optional:

- some plastic wrap

Shopping list

- 2 large **oranges** or 3 small oranges, seedless if possible (these should be edible, not juicing oranges)
- 1 tablespoon of **sugar** (preferably brown sugar, but white granulated sugar will do)
- ½ teaspoon of **cinnamon** (if you do not like cinnamon, you can substitute a few mint leaves cut into thin strips)
- 1 tablespoon of **orange flower water** (you will find it in the supermarket or in an Oriental grocery store) or 1 tablespoon of rum

Method

Wash the oranges thoroughly in cold water and dry them. Remove three long strips of peel (zests) from one orange, using the potato peeler. Cut them into thin strips about 1/8 inch (1 millimeter) in width. Cut off the top and bottom of each orange then remove the peel, using the knife and cutting slightly into the flesh, so that none of the white pulpy layer remains.

Cut each orange into 4 or 5 slices horizontally (i.e. cutting across the segments). Put half of the slices on each plate. Sprinkle them with sugar and cinnamon. Pour the orange flower water over them and decorate with the zests of orange. Leave the

plates in the refrigerator for at least 2 hours to allow the flavors to mingle thoroughly.

Advance preparation
This salad can be prepared the day before. Keep it in the refrigerator, covered with plastic wrap.

Puff pastries with raspberries and cream

An attractive-looking dessert, smooth, crunchy, and cool.

How long it will take

5 minutes' preparation
+ 10 minutes' cooking time

The equipment you need

· baking parchment roll or sheet
· 1 bottle
· 1 small bowl
· 1 knife
· 1 oven
· 1 baking tray or 1 ovenproof broiler pan
· 1 tablespoon

Shopping list

· 1 package of frozen **puff pastry**
· about 40 **raspberries** (a pack weighing around 4 ounces (125 grams))
· 4 tablespoons of **heavy cream**
· 2 tablespoons of **sugar**

Method

Defrost the package of puff pastry in the microwave to allow it to soften and make it easier to roll out (or remove from the refrigerator if you have placed it there the day before). Remove from the oven the baking tray or broiler pan on which you intend to cook the pastries and line with parchment paper. Set the oven to 400 °F. It takes 20 minutes for an electric oven to heat up, 10 minutes for a gas oven (some ovens have a light which goes off when the desired temperature has been reached). Roll out the dough using the bottle. Place the small bowl rim on the dough, very near the edge, and press hard to cut out a circular piece. If it does not come away cleanly, cut it out with a knife. Repeat this step for the second pastry. Remove the excess dough. When the oven has reached the right temperature, place the dough circles on the baking tray or broiler pan and put them in the oven.

Leave them to bake for 10 minutes. During this time, mix the heavy cream with the sugar in the bowl until it is a stiff cream. If the pastry begins to burn, turn down the oven to 350 °F. When they are ready, remove the dough circles from the oven and slide them onto the plates. Allow them to cool. Spread half of the cream on each circle, then put half of the raspberries on top. It's ready.

Strawberries and banana envelopes

This method of cooking in foil packages retains the flavors of the fruits and makes them soft and creamy.

How long it will take

15 minutes' preparation
+ 15 minutes' cooking time

The equipment you need

· 1 oven
· 1 baking tray or ovenproof broiler pan
· 1 knife
· 1 clean dish towel or some paper towels
· 1 tablespoon
· 3 feet (1 meter) of aluminum foil

Shopping list

· 10 **strawberries** (or 20 raspberries)
· 1 **banana**
· 1 knob of **butter** (a piece the size of a walnut)
· 2 tablespoons of **sugar**
Optional:
· 2 **mint** leaves

Method

Remove from the oven the baking tray or broiler pan on which you intend to cook the envelopes. Set the oven to 450 °F. It takes about 20 minutes for an electric oven to heat up, 10 minutes for a gas oven (some ovens have a light to indicate when the desired temperature has been reached). Peel the banana and cut it into sections of about 1/4 inch (5 millimeters). Wash the strawberries quickly in cold water and dry them with a dish towel or some paper towels. Cut them in half from top to bottom. If you are using raspberries, leave them just as they are. Tear the aluminum foil to obtain 2 pieces each 18 inches (50 centimeters) long.

Lay the first piece of foil on a flat, clean surface, shiny side down. Put half of the knob of butter on it and spread it gently with a paper towel, leaving a margin of roughly 1 1/2 inches (4 centimeters) all around. Place the fruits on the buttered area, and sprinkle 1 tablespoon of sugar over them. Wrap up the fruit by folding over the edges of the aluminum foil several times, so that the envelope is hermetically sealed (it is vital to keep all the flavor in). Wrap up the second envelope in the same way. Place both envelopes on the baking tray and put them in the oven. Leave them to cook 15 minutes. Then gently remove them from the oven and put one on each plate. Open them up with a knife. If desi-

red, decorate with 1 leaf of mint, and serve immediately.

Advance preparation
You can prepare the envelopes earlier in the evening, before your guest arrives. All you need do then is put them in the oven.

Apple and date crumble with coconut

A really delicious, slightly exotic version of a classic dessert.

How long it will take

How long it will take
30 minutes' preparation
+ 30 minutes' cooking time

The equipment you need

• 1 oven
• 1 small, sharp knife
• 1 potato peeler
• 1 ovenproof dish for 2 persons
• 1 tablespoon
• 1 bowl for preparing the crumble
• 1 measuring cup
• 1 clean dish towel or some paper towels
Optional:
• some aluminum foil or some plastic
  wrap

Shopping list

• 1 ½ **apples** (golden delicious would be
  a suitable choice)
• 8 **dates** (including 2 for decoration)
• ½ cup of flaked **coconut**
• ½ stick (50 grams) of **butter**
• ½ cup of all-purpose **flour**
• ½ cup of **superfine sugar** (to be found
  on the baking shelf in the supermarket)

Method

Set the oven to 350 °F. It takes about 20 minutes for an electric oven to heat up,
10 minutes for a gas oven (some ovens have a light to indicate when the desired
temperature has been reached). Cut the apples into segments. Peel them with the
potato peeler and remove the core from each segment using the knife. Then cut
each segment into small pieces. Remove the pits from the dates, then cut the dates
in half. Arrange the apples and 12 date halves in the ovenproof dish (set 2 dates
aside for decoration).

If the dish is rather big for the amount of fruit, push it together on one side of the dish and leave part of the dish empty. Cut the butter into small pieces. Place the butter, the flour, the sugar, and the coconut in the bowl. Knead the ingredients with your fingers, making sure you break down the pieces of butter, until the flour, the sugar, and the coconut are fully blended in. The mixture should be fairly grainy; do not try to obtain a very smooth result. Spread this mixture over the fruit to form a crust. When the oven is fully heated, put the dish inside and leave it to cook about 30 minutes, by which time the crust should be a golden color. Take a look occasionally to make sure it is not getting too brown. If it is, lower the temperature to 300 °F and let it continue to cook. If, on the other hand, the crust is not golden after 20 minutes, increase the temperature to 400 °F. When it is done, remove the dish from the oven using an oven glove to protect yourself. Serve out half of the crumble onto each plate, trying to keep the crumble uppermost. Decorate each plate with 1 date and allow to cool 5 minutes before serving.

Advance preparation

You can prepare the crumble the day before, without cooking it. In this case, mix some lemon juice in with the fruit, to prevent it from oxidizing and going brown. Keep the crumble in the refrigerator, having covered it with aluminum foil or plastic wrap.

Strawberry fruit salad with honey, lemon, and mint

The honey gives the strawberries an alluring shine; the mint adds a touch of coolness.

How long it will take

20 minutes

The equipment you need

· 1 salad bowl
· 1 dish towel or some paper towels
· 1 knife
· 1 tablespoon
Optional:
· 1 lemon squeezer
· 1 pair of scissors for cutting up the mint

Shopping list

· ½ pound (250 grams) of **strawberries**
· ½ **lemon**
· 1 tablespoon of **liquid honey**
· 8 **mint leaves**

Method

Squeeze the 1/2 lemon over the salad bowl. Remove any pits. Pour the honey in with the lemon juice and mix well. Quickly wash the strawberries in cold water, then dry them with a dish towel or some paper towels. Remove the stems, then cut the strawberries in half from top to bottom. Put them in the salad bowl and turn gently with the tablespoon to coat them in the honey and lemon sauce. Wash and wipe the mint leaves. Keep 2 aside for decoration and cut the others into thin strips with the knife or scissors. Distribute the cut mint over the salad and arrange the 2 whole leaves on top.

Advance preparation
This dessert can be prepared several hours before the guest arrives. Keep it in the refrigerator.

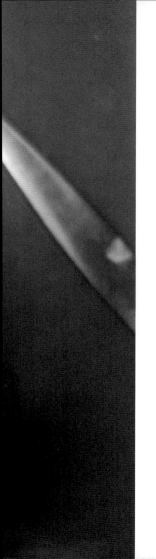

Breakfast

Personal experiences

Joanna almost knocked over the boiled eggs in my bed. Frankly, I would not have held it against her.
Billy, 20, website designer

It's cool to lie in bed in the morning, drinking a cup of coffee and enjoying a cuddle.
Mickey, 23, mechanic

I don't know if it was my cooking that made Karen snore. In any case, next morning I was a real gentleman: I didn't mention it.
Clark, 48, fireman

I even squeezed
the oranges and buttered
her bread. Something tells
me Marie will be back.
**John, 31, communications
advisor**

A festive
meal, a guest for
the night…
**Tim, 33,
draftsman**

To
wake a sleeping
beauty, I know nothing
better than a nice break-
fast in bed.
**Edward, 27,
accountant**

Getting the breakfast right

The supper persuaded her to stay? The aim of breakfast should be to make her want to come again...

There are two likely scenarios:
· a quick breakfast before rushing off to work;
· a relaxed breakfast, for example at the weekend.

For the quick version

Drinks

· Have some good quality **fruit juice** handy: conventional orange juice or, for something more original, grapefruit or apple juice.

· Where **tea** is concerned, you can get teabags with attractive-sounding names (English breakfast, orange pekoe, or Earl Grey, for example).

· When it comes to **coffee**, everything depends on your equipment. If you only have a saucepan, you'll have to make instant coffee. If you have a coffeemaker, make it the way you would normally.

· Make sure you have some **sugar**, granulated or in lump form, and some **milk**, if she uses it (semi-skimmed if she's sensitive about her figure).

Food

· If you are using **bread** left over from the evening before, keep it in a plastic bag or wrapped in a dish towel to stop it from drying out, and toast it next morning. If you don't have a toaster, put it under the broiler (making sure it doesn't burn).

· If you are up to it, go out and buy some fresh bread or some **pastries** (dough-nuts, buns, Danish pastries, for example); you'll be greeted like a returning hero.

· It's a good idea to offer a choice of **jams, some honey**... and some **butter. Put the jams on the table in their original jars, with a separate spoon for each one.** The butter can be presented in a proper butter dish, or on a small plate.

· If you really want to please your guest, a quick and easy solution is **yogurt** with **honey** (see page 155).

For a more relaxed breakfast

This is the ideal situation: take your time and sit down to breakfast together...

Drinks

- **Fruit juices:** you can either buy them (see quick breakfast section) or, if you have a lemon squeezer, you can make fresh orange juice, which is excellent and fun to do.
- **Tea, coffee, sugar, milk:** see quick breakfast section.

Food

In addition to **bread, butter** and different **jams**, you can prolong the pleasure by offering:
- **yogurts** or **cottage cheese**;
- **fruit**;
- **cheese** (but avoid anything with a strong smell);
- **ham**;
- **cereals** of the muesli or crunchy type with milk (which girls are very fond of);
- **eggs** (which you will, of course, have to cook: see recipe on page 156).

Yogurt with honey

Very simple... but very sexy!

How long it will take

5 minutes

The equipment you need

· 2 bowls
· 1 tablespoon

Shopping list

· about 8 ounces (250 grams) of **yogurt**;
  for a lighter version of the recipe, buy
  yogurt with 0 % fat content
· 4 tablespoons of **liquid honey**
Optional:
· 6 **walnut kernels** (the edible part of the
  nut which remains when you remove the
  shell; you will find them on the baking
  shelf in the supermarket, or with the
  dried fruit)

Method

Put half of the yogurt in each bowl. Pour 2 tablespoons of honey on top; do not mix it in. If you wish, you can also break the walnut kernels into four and place them on top of the cheese, around the honey. It's as simple as that.

Boiled eggs with toast strips

The strips of buttered toast are for dipping in the egg yolk. Delicious.

How long it will take

10 minutes

The equipment you need

• 1 knife
• 2-4 egg cups or some aluminum foil
• 1 saucepan
• 1 cooktop
• 1 tablespoon
• 1 teaspoon
Optional:
• 1 toaster or an oven

Shopping list

• 2 to 4 **eggs** depending how hungry you are (the fresher the eggs the better; in any case, they should not be more than 10 days old)
• **sliced bread** (allow for four toast strips per egg)
• **butter**
• **salt**

Method

The bread can be toasted. Butter it, then cut it into thin strips. Take the eggs out of the refrigerator. Get out egg cups for serving the eggs in; this is the simplest method. Otherwise, you can shape some aluminum foil into little "nests" for holding the eggs and preventing them from rolling around. Stand the egg cups on plates. Put the eggs in the saucepan and fill it with water, so that the eggs are covered. Put the saucepan on to boil. At first, very small bubbles will form. When they become larger, time the eggs to cook 3 minutes, then remove them from the water using the tablespoon.

Put the eggs in the egg cups, pointed end up. Using the knife or a teaspoon, tap each egg about 1/8 inch (1 centimeter) from the top to break the shell. Now, using the knife, cut off the top of each egg and put the piece you have removed on the side of the plate. Put the toast strips on the plates around the eggs. Dip 1 into each egg, breaking the white to reach the yolk and serve.

Recipes you can make with limited equipment

You don't have a cooktop or an oven (so you can only serve cold dishes)

You have a cooktop (but no oven)

You have an oven (but no cooktop)

The genesis of this book

nicole.seeman@laposte.net

Is there anything more appealing and moving for a woman than to be invited to dinner by a man who has done the cooking himself? This question occurred to Nicole on one unforgettable occasion when she received just such an invitation. We know the answer... Nicole Seeman is neither a great chef nor a catering professional, but she does have a passion for good food. The walls of her living room are covered with restaurant menus, souvenirs of memorable meals and old recipes hunted down at flea markets. Over the last 15 years, she has taken many cooking courses with a view to giving pleasure to those around her. And while delighting her boyfriends, she had the idea of giving them a helping hand. Her philosophy? You don't need to be talented or very experienced to produce enjoyable dishes. She therefore tracked down a number of clueless guinea pigs (not a particularly difficult exercise) with a view to passing on the tricks and skills she had learned. The recipes in this book have been tested by genuine out-and-out beginners. Special thanks should go to Jean-Luc, who was prepared to taste everything without complaining, including the recipes that had not yet been perfected, and to Michel, for trying them out himself and asking the kind of questions you would expect from a nonpracticing cook (he has since become a master of scallops with pastis).

Raphaële Vidaling, also a keen cook, took the photographs—her first venture in this field, since her specialty is literature. In her first novel (*Plusieurs fois par moi*, published by Grasset), she had created the character "mwfm" (the "man who feeds me"). So she and Nicole were almost destined to work together on this project...

raphaele.vidaling@laposte.net